vegan
Morning
♥Noon
& Night
& everything in between

100+

whole food
gluten free
recipes

BY: BECKY HUNT

Outskirts Press, Inc.
http://www.outskirtspress.com

Paperback ISBN: 978-1-9772-0113-3
Hardback ISBN: 978-1-9772-0132-4

Cover Photo © 2018 Becky Hunt

Outskirts Press and the "OP" logo are trademarks belonging to Outskirts Press, Inc.

PRINTED IN THE UNITED STATES OF AMERICA

This book is dedicated to my two precious girls
Gracia & Emilia, for making me want to
be brave and follow my dreams.

Spread Some
Happy!
♡

Betty

TABLE OF CONTENTS

Introduction

The Recipes

Hi, I'm Becky!

Going Vegan was a huge turning point in my life. Just having been diagnosed with Stage 3 Melanoma Cancer, about to have several surgeries and then go right into two years of treatment, I knew my health needed to be number one. As with most critical turning points, they follow a longer story. Here's that story.

Like most kids in the Midwest, I grew up on casseroles filled with meats and cheeses, roasts, hot dogs cut up in my Mac & Cheese and sneaking cookie dough when mom wasn't looking while she made cookies, your stereotypical American kid diet.

My diagnosis of type 1 diabetes came at just 13 years old. Without any history of diabetes in my family, I was the experiment child for many endocrinologists throughout my teenage years. I quickly learned a lot about food and carbohydrates but also gained 70 pounds in as little as 2 years.

Early in my diabetes journey, my doctors and dietitians instructed me to adjust my food/carbohydrate intake to balance a fixed insulin dose to keep my blood sugars stable. This method resulted in my weight going up and down for years and me being confused as to what was going on with my body. I tried cutting calories dramatically, exercising until I was exhausted, and getting to the point I could see my ribs in the mirror. Finally, that low number on the scale took me by surprise. As depression started kicking in, my weight went back up. My body was drained, weak, tired, DONE.

Then I married the most amazing man that loved every part of me. We had a little girl with a special heart named Gracie. August 2nd, 2012, she came into this world with dark hair and beautiful blue eyes.

She was born with only half of a heart; a Congenital Heart Defect called Hypoplastic Left Heart Syndrome. Her incredible story is a WHOLE book I need to write someday but our time with her was cut short to only 82 days. After she passed away, you can imagine I was in a profoundly dark place. I couldn't physically eat or sleep but I did find that I wanted to be in the kitchen all the time just baking. So I baked, and I baked until the cakes and cupcakes were overflowing.

I had a serious passion for creating recipes and making tummies happy. I knew I needed to do something with this passion and started a legacy for my Gracie with a non-profit organization called Cakes From Grace. It's mission, donating cakes to kiddos, just like Gracie, born with heart defects. By making a custom dream cake and bringing it to the hospital while they wait for a heart transplant, or to celebrate coming home after a big surgery. Whatever the occasion was, I help them celebrate their life.

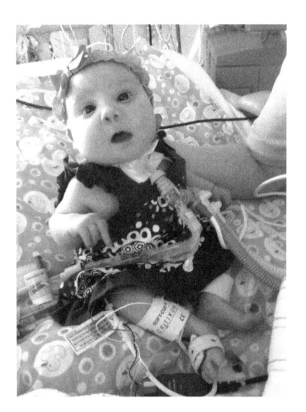

When Gracie's sister was born in 2014, I felt a small piece of my broken heart grew back into place. Emilia Grace, my rainbow baby, was my saving Grace. She saved me in so many ways. I wanted to be a stronger and more fearless Mommy for her.

Having a passion for baking and a recipe list a mile long, I had to start sharing some of my secrets. Thus, I started a YouTube channel, Becky Bakes. I created video tutorials of many of my healthier recipes, sort of like a baking show.

Then in May of 2015, my world came crashing down yet again. I heard the words that no 28-year-old Mom should ever hear - "You have Cancer."

This news was a huge turning point for me. A huge awakening. One of those times where you question everything in your life, re-prioritize everything and STOP to hold your loved ones even closer and longer than you ever have before.

I did what most would do after getting a new diagnosis, Google it and find dozens of books on it. Find out what you can do to fix it. I did endless amounts of research and knew the first thing I needed to do was to take out all animal products from my diet completely. Go Vegan overnight.

I told my family what I was doing and why I was doing it and they all supported me, and I'm thankful. It was tough, I'm not going to lie, especially when it came to CHEESE. But I was determined to create an alternative. When I so badly wanted cheese I thought about my daughter, I thought about the Cancer that LOVES animal products. It was an easy decision to make this change so that I could be here for Emilia tomorrow and the next day.

Here I am 3 years later, 30 pounds down, healthier, more fit, and happier than I ever remember being. Not to mention, no Cancer in sight!

When people ask me how I've stayed Vegan for so long, I tell them that you have to find a reason why YOU want to be Vegan. A reason for YOU as an individual. Do your own research and find out if it's right for you. For me, I couldn't find a reason NOT to be Vegan. To better my insulin sensitivity for my diabetes, to free myself from eating disorders and restriction, to save the animals and our environment we live in, to jump higher, run faster, and live Cancer free. Whatever your reason, find it.

The other things I recommend, find some staple recipes that you absolutely LOVE. And that's why I wrote this book. It took me three years to create my favorite Vegan meals and staples. And now it's time to share them with YOU.

Here I am 3 years later, 30 pounds down, healthier, more fit, and happier then I ever remember being.

WRITING THE BOOK

If you learn one thing about me, it would be that if I set my mind and heart on something, I make it happen. No doubt.

I've always loved writing. Stories, recipes, thoughts, feelings, all of it.

I ended a toxic chapter in my life in 2017. 2018 was going to be MY year to do things MY way. To take care of myself and focus on what I'm most passionate about. Baking and creating really yummy and nutritionally dense recipes.

For many years I have created, tested and compiled hundreds of Vegan recipes. I've also always wanted to write and publish my own book. I decided that 2018 was going to be the year I was going to make that dream a reality.

In January of 2018, I started writing my recipes down. Before that, I would toss this in and that in, never really measuring. Testing out new recipes, re-testing old ones. Taking photos of every dish along the way. I condensed it down to my top 103 recipes.

Taking seven months focusing on my passion and spending a lot of time in the kitchen, made me feel free. Free to be Becky and doing what I love. It's been a huge turning point. The first turning point in my life that has been positive and healing.

This book is a reflection of me. It has me written all over it, and I'm proud of that. You'll also notice a lot of pink. That's for my Gracie. Her best color was pink, and if you flip through to my pretty in pink pitaya bowl or take a look at my shoes on the cover of this book, that's what we call "Gracie Pink" because bright pink was always my Gracie Girl's best color.

She would positively light up in it!

For Emilia, I had to make a pink donut with rainbow sprinkles JUST for her.

My girls are all over this book, which makes it so special to me.

As you go through the recipes and pages of this book, I hope that your heart and tummies will fill with joy.

This book is a
reflection of me.
It has me written all over it.

100% Plant-Based, Vegan Ingredients

You will not find any animal products whatsoever in this book. No meat, no fish, no eggs, no dairy, no honey. Just straight up food that grows from the Earth.

Whole Food Ingredients

It was my number one priority to make every recipe from whole and unprocessed ingredients as best I could. Fruits, Vegetables, Grains, Nuts and Seeds in the their whole form. In these recipes, you will find very few minimally processed ingredients.

Recipes Making Other Recipes

Many of the recipes in this cookbook, such as sauces, will be used to make multiple recipes. For example, you'll see my mozzarella cheese will show up in sandwich and pizza recipes. My BBQ chickpeas will be on pizza and nourish bowls. I wanted there to be recipes you could make again and again, using them in endless amounts of ways. I hope these recipes will become staples in your cooking!

Recipes For Everyone, Every Age!

Who are these recipes for you ask? For every Vegan, want-to-be Vegan, on-the-fence and looking into possibly becoming Vegan, and every non-vegan. My husband is a meat lover and has devoured all 103 of these recipes gladly, happily! My four-year-old daughter was also my inspiration behind the kid-friendly recipes, especially the chicken-less chickpea nuggets!

Superfoods

So what's a superfood? I love to pack my meals with superfoods. I define them as super duper densely packed nutritious foods and ingredients that will set your body on fire! In the best way possible, that is! These foods are so healing and energizing for your body. They help remove toxins, fight cancer and give your body so much life and love. You can read more about my favorite superfoods on pages 14-19.

WHAT YOU WON'T FIND IN THIS BOOK

Gluten

I decided to make everything in this book gluten-free. I have found for myself that I have a sensitivity to gluten. An inflammatory response that is not kind to my digestion. Whether you have celiac disease or just a minor sensitivity, everything in this book is for you too!

Artificial or Refined Anything

No artificial ingredients; sweeteners, sugars, preservatives, flavors, chemicals. Everything is REAL. Just REAL food. Artificial ingredients confuse your body because it doesn't recognize them. How do I process this thing, how do I use it? In fact, having something with artificial sweeteners in it tricks your body into thinking it's receiving sugar, but because it's "sugar-free" your body continues to ask for sugar because it's waiting for it. This response is when those cravings kick in, and you want to have more. Your body is smart, but it won't recognize fake things.

A Diet Plan

Vegan Morning, Noon and Night is by no means a diet book. It is a healthy, plant-based cookbook made with natural, nutritionally dense foods picked from the earth to provide your body with the vitamins and minerals it desires and needs to thrive. Your body's personal needs are going to be different from your brother's needs and your Mom's needs. Your preferences are going to be different. You might enjoy snacks in between meals while your brother likes to eat just 2 or 3 solid meals a day. Listen to your body, write down how it's feeling, you got this!!

Calorie Counting

I put a lot of thought into whether I should include nutrition facts, macronutrients and calories with every recipe. Coming from a background of eating disorders, as I explained on page 7, numbers and counting have become something very toxic to me, something that causes anxiety for a lot of people.

I think it's very important for people to practice listening to their bodies and eating intuitively.

Your body is so FLIPPING amazing, and it knows what you need. Your body is so good at sending you cues that you need to eat, such as a grumble in your belly. Craving something sweet? That's your body telling you it needs vitamins from fresh naturally sweet fruit. Craving something meaty? Another cue from your body, possibly needing iron from beans and legumes.

The way I see it, God placed trees in the ground with sweet and juicy fruit, grains and herbs to grow up from the soil to nourish our bodies, to give us energy, to keep sickness and disease away. If you've ever asked your body, "what am I craving?" or sat down to a meal and savored every bite and stopped eating when your body told you to stop, then you understand. It's sending a cue, "This doesn't taste good anymore. I'm done. I've had enough."

If not, try it sometime.

I lost 30 pounds only after I stopped stressing about and counting calories. Try it and if you'd still like to count everything, if that helps you know you're getting every nutrient in, AWESOME! Go for it friend! There are a ton of apps for that!

One of my favorite quotes is from Dr. Mark Hyman "Food is not just calories, it is information. It talks to your DNA and tells it what to do. The most powerful tool to change your health, environment and entire world is your fork."

Words to live by!

BACK TO BASICS

Freezing Bananas

It might not sound like the most complicated thing in the world but a lot of people will goof this part up.
#1 PEEL the banana before tossing it in the freezer.
#2 To keep the bananas from sticking to each other, place the bananas on a baking sheet lined with parchment paper, freeze them on the sheet THEN place them in whatever container you want to keep them in and have them on hand whenever you need!

Double Boiler

A double boiler is basically two saucepans fitted on top of one another. The larger, bottom saucepan is partially filled with water brought to a simmer. The inner saucepan (or just using a glass bowl), laid on top of the larger pan, provides indirect heat to melt or cook sauces, chocolates, etc.

Aquafaba

What is it? Well, you know the liquid you drain from the can of chickpeas (garbanzo beans)? That is called "aquafaba". It's this magical liquid that can do amazing things! A lot of fancy desserts call for whipped egg whites (or meringue) to make fluffy mousse's or a lemon meringue pie, well this will do the same thing. YES! In fact, whenever I open a can of chickpeas, I save the liquid in a jar and keep it in the fridge for when a recipe calls for it. Just whip it up whenever you need!

Soaking Cashews

Many of my sauces call for soaked cashews. Soaking cashews make for a creamy and thick dressing or sauce without having to use any dairy products. So here is how to do it. However many cashews a recipe calls for, measure that out and place them in a bowl. Cover the cashews with water by an inch or two. Let these sit ideally overnight. If you forget to set them up the night before, cover them with boiling water for at least 4 hours.

Cooking Quinoa

Some recipes call for prepared quinoa. Well here is my tried and true way of making it. Cooking Quinoa is a 1:2 ratio. 1 Cup dry quinoa + 2 Cups water or 1/2 cup dry quinoa + 1 Cup water, you get the idea. Whatever amount you are making, place the quinoa and water in a pot on the stove and bring to a boil. Turn off the burner and cover the pot with a lid and let it stand on the stove as is for 15-20 minutes. Yes, turning off the burner is critical otherwise, your quinoa will overcook and stick the bottom of the pan. Also, don't touch it, don't stir it, just back off and let it do its thang!

STAPLES IN THE KITCHEN

EQUIPMENT

Before you dive into the recipes and stock up on ingredients, there are a few things you will want to check and make sure you have. You'll find that most of the recipes in this book do not require more than a spatula, measuring spoons, cups, a good knife and mixin' bowls, but there are a few staples and tools that are must-haves in the kitchen!

High Speed Blender

The best investment I ever made was hands down my Vitamix 5200 blender. I've had mine for seven years, and she has never let me down. Some other brands that I would recommend are a Blendtec and a Ninja. I can't promise you PERFECT results from these, but they should do the job! Why not a regular $20 blender? Let's just say it won't be able to handle the job, and you may find yourself back at the supermarket buying another blender.

Food Processor

Although the high-speed blender can do the same job as a food processor, sometimes it's just easier to do some things with a food processor, mostly because it's easier to pulse, scrape the sides when needed, but also handy for recipes that only require a quick chop and mix.

Spiralizer

A spiralizer is the tool that will transform your vegetables into long pasta-like noodles! I have a few pasta recipes that do call for spiralized zucchini noodles, but if you don't have one, no worries, grab a vegetable peeler and go to town! You might have thicker noodles, but it works just as well.

Stand Mixer or Hand Mixer

My fancy Kitchen Aid Mixer, although loved in my kitchen, is not a requirement for these recipes. A good old hand mixer with a whisk attachment will do just fine!

Instant Pot

The day I got my Instant Pot, I was forever changed as a busy working Mom who does forget about dinner from time to time. Gone are the days I use a slow cooker thinking about what's for dinner at 8:00 in the morning and filling a pot before I even start the day. A close second to my favorite tool in the kitchen, this baby is a lifesaver. Plopping ingredients in, setting it for 15-25 minutes and BAM dinner is done! Don't have an instant pot? I highly recommend getting in on a black Friday sale like I did, but it's not necessary to have one. I include a bunch of recipes that call for an instant pot, but you'll be happy to hear that I also include the stove top version for all but my risotto recipe.

Silpat Silicone Baking Mat

A non-stick mat that I use to make my oil-free french fries. A definite must for roasting anything without oil!

Popcorn Popper

No matter how you pop them, you'll need something to pop your popcorn for the epic caramel popcorn on page 109. My favorite? The good old whirly pop! You could also use an air popper or even a saucepan with a lid.

THE PANTRY

I thought I would include some information about a few of the ingredients in this cookbook that most people haven't heard of or know little about. The more you know about your food, the more motivated you'll be to nourish your body with the right foods and in turn, the better you will feel, right?

Pink Himalayan Sea Salt

You'll find that just about every recipe includes "sea salt." You can use just simple sea salt, which has great benefits as is. But for me, the only kind of sea salt I use is Himalayan Pink Salt. It's as unrefined and pure as they come. Its high iron content is a nutrient some vegans don't get enough of. It helps regulate electrolytes in the body, regulate blood pressure and aids in muscle recovery. So if you can, make your sea salt Himalayan!

Vanilla

Powder vs. extract. Why do I prefer the powder version? No alcohol. But the powder version can be more expensive and harder to find. Feel free to use the extract instead.

Nut Butters

I use three different kinds of nut butter in this book, almond, peanut, and cashew. To keep nut butter as clean and nutritionally dense as possible, make sure the only ingredient listed is almonds, peanuts, or cashews. No added salt, no oil, no sugar. Buying them "raw" is even better, but not always easy to find. Have a nut allergy? You can substitute any nut butter in any recipe with coconut butter or sunflower seed butter (sun butter).

Nut Milks

Most all my recipes that call for milk suggest you use a "nut milk of your choosing." In my personal opinion, all nut milk comes out with the same result, except for full fat, canned coconut milk. So when creating these recipes choose a nut milk that you like most. Almond, Soy, Cashew, Hazelnut, Hemp, Macadamia (my fave), or even rice milk. Try different kinds, they all taste a little different, find what you like.

Sweeteners

I have completely replaced all refined sugars in my kitchen and only use these three as they are the purest you can find. They are also all lower on the glycemic index (better for blood sugar levels).

#1 Pure Maple Syrup (straight from the maple tree)

#2 Monkfruit (I buy mine online)

#3 Coconut Palm Sugar (great alternative to granulated sugar)

Ground Flax Seeds

High in Omega-3 essential fatty acids (key for heart health). You can get these seeds in its whole form of course, but the recipes included in this book require them to be ground. You can either buy them already ground or grind up a handful at a time in a coffee grinder. Keep stored in the fridge.

Cacao Powder and Nibs

My favorite thing in the world is Chocolate. Cacao is chocolate in it's rawest form. Nibs are the cacao in its whole form (my favorite crunchy chocolate chip-like topping), and the powder is the ground up version. So what's the difference between that and cocoa powder? Cocoa powder is the processed (heated up) version of cacao. It still has great benefits but not as many, and that's why I prefer cacao. Not only is Cacao the highest source of plant-based iron you can find but it also contains more calcium than cows milk, YEAH!

Arrowroot Flour

Also known as Arrowroot "starch." Arrowroot is my number one go-to when things need to be well, thicker! I prefer arrowroot over other starches because it thickens at a lower temperature and it's higher in fiber making it easily digestible.

Almond Flour

Almond flour is a fabulous replacement for flour. It's gluten-free, full of nutrients, and found in most stores. You may find almond "meal" which is great for most recipes, but when it comes to baking, you'll want a finely ground flour.

Oat Flour

My favorite flour alternative for everything. Why? Because I can buy my oats in bulk and make it myself! Say WHAT?! You can buy oat flour of course, but you'll save a lot more money when you grind it yourself. How? Place a few cups of whole oats in your high-speed blender and blend away until you have a flour!

Coconut Flour

Essentially dried coconut in powdered form. It's fabulous for baking, super absorbent and can create a softer, denser product.

Nutritional Yeast

In my book, this is a super duper must-have in your kitchen! But is it yeast? It's a deactivated yeast that is super rich in Vitamin B12, which is another nutrient that some vegans are deficient in if you don't supplement. For me, this is the easiest nutrient to get in because Nutritional Yeast is so flippin' good! You'll find that I put this ingredient in most of my recipes that require a cheesy flavor! So it is an absolute MUST in your pantry! Where can you find it? You can usually find it in the bulk aisle at your local grocer or any health foods store, or well, Amazon!

Hemp Heart Seeds

Hemp is the seed that has my heart! I sprinkle these babies on anything and everything sweet or savory. These seeds do a great job reducing inflammation, lowering blood pressure and heart disease risk. Not to mention they are super high in protein!

Spirulina Powder

Spirulina powder is a natural algae with super potent nutrients, high in protein and antioxidants. It may be very green (both in color and taste) but the Cancer-fighting benefits alone win me over. You'll find it in a few smoothie recipes, so it's always an optional ingredient.

Chia Seeds

"You got something there in your teeth." Yeah, that will happen with chia seeds, but I'll tell you the benefits are so worth it. High in omega-3's, iron, calcium, and fiber. Once these babies hit liquid, they expand so they are great for thickening just about anything and are pretty fun to eat too. Just check your teeth before going into that meeting!

Unrefined Coconut Oil

You'll find that just about every recipe does not include any oil at all. Oils are not a whole food and are stripped away from its whole, natural form where the majority of nutrients rest. Oil is completely unnecessary when it comes to cooking, but when it comes to baking that's an entirely different thing. Baking is a science. And in my many many years of scientific study, I have found that you need that added fat to make your cakes and cookies to turn out the way that they should. And as a whole food Vegan, I prefer to use unrefined coconut oil not only for its health benefits but also because it works just as beautifully as butter does.

Maca Powder

Not only does Maca improve your energy, mood, and memory, it's also known to increase libido and fertility. It also gives your food a caramel-like taste!

Matcha Powder

I am a lover of all things Matcha! High in antioxidants, strengthens your immune system, boosts memory and concentration, an energy powerhouse and my absolute favorite perk; Catechins (ECG's) to fight off Cancer *YEAH*

Plant-Based Protein Powder

Many of the smoothies and ice cream bowls in this book call for a Plant-Based Protein Powder, but it is always an optional ingredient. If you're like me and you like to have a diet a bit higher in protein, then add it, but it's not necessary. You can find dairy free, whey free, vegan-friendly protein powders just about anywhere these days. Vega and Sun Warrior are my top 2 favorite brands. For the recipes in this book, you will need a vanilla flavor. Find one you love!

Acai

My obsession with acai began many years ago when my life forever changed with my first acai bowl experience. It was heaven on earth. Blended in a beautiful bowl the benefits are endless. Having the highest antioxidants you can find among all fruits and vegetables; it can help with inflammation, neurological diseases, allergies, digestion issues, cellular health and the immune system. You can find acai both in powder form or in the frozen food isle packed in a little, frozen pouch.

Dragonfruit

I discovered pitaya bowls while in California, and my life forever changed yet again. The color is beyond perfect and makes me smile. Dragon fruit (the ingredient in a pitaya bowl that makes everything Gracie Pink) is fantastic for good heart health and has cancer-fighting superpowers. Like acai, you can find this in powder and frozen pouches. The powder makes for excellent food coloring when you need a little pink or purple (acai) frosting!

Breakfast

ACAI BOWL

INGREDIENTS

1/2 Cup Frozen Mango
1/2 Cup Frozen Berries
2 Frozen Bananas
2 Tbsp Acai Powder or 1
Packet of Frozen Acai
1 Cup Coconut Water

OPTIONAL TOPPINGS:
Cacao Nibs
Coconut Strips
Hemp Heart Seeds
Berries
Banana
Goji Berries
Chia Seeds
Chopped Dates
Rawnola or Granola
Nuts & Seeds
Drizzle of Nut Butter

INSTRUCTIONS

1. Place all ingredients into a high speed blender.
2. Blend until smooth like soft serve ice cream.
3. Pour out into a bowl and place any toppings of your choosing on top.

Tip: For a lower sugar version, just replace 1 banana with 1 cup of frozen cauliflower

BLUEBERRY BANANA MUFFINS

PREP
10 MINS

COOK
20 MINS

MAKES
DOZEN

INGREDIENTS

1 Tbsp Baking Powder
1 1/2 Cups Oat Flour
1 Ripe Banana
3/4 Cup Nut Milk of Choice
1 tsp Vanilla Extract
1/2 Cup Coconut Palm Sugar
1 Cup Frozen Blueberries

INSTRUCTIONS

1. In a large bowl, mix your oat flour and baking powder together.
2. Place the remaining ingredients (except for the blueberries) into a blender or food processor and blend until smooth.
3. Add your wet mixture to the flour and baking soda. Mix with a spatula until all ingredients are wet and incorporated.
4. Fold in your frozen blueberries without over mixing.
5. Line your muffin pan with cupcake liners.
6. Scoop your batter evenly between 12 liners.
7. Place in the oven at 350F for 20-25 minutes or until a toothpick inserted comes out clean.
8. Let muffins cool for 15 minutes before enjoying.

CRUNCHY RAWNOLA

PREP
10 MINS

SERVES
4

8 Medjool Dates, pitted
1/2 Cup Rolled Oats
1/2 Cup Buckwheat Groats
1/8 tsp Cinnamon

INSTRUCTIONS

1. Place all ingredients into a high speed blender or food processor.
2. Pulse until just combined.
3. Sprinkle over banana nice cream or eat by the spoonful!

COOL CREAMY CHOCOLATE NICE CREAM

PREP
10 MINS

SERVES
ONE

3 Frozen Bananas
2 Tbsp Cacao Powder
1/4 Cup Nut Milk of Choice

TOPPINGS:
1/3 cup of Crunchy Rawnola
(recipe above)
1/2 Tbsp Cacao Nibs

INSTRUCTIONS

1. Place bananas, cacao powder, and milk into a high speed blender or food processor.
2. Blend until smooth like a soft serve ice cream.
3. Top with crunchy rawnola and cacao nibs or whatever you so wish.

Tip: For a lower sugar version,
just replace 1 banana with
1 cup of frozen cauliflower

OVERNIGHT OATS BASE

3/4 Cup Rolled Oats
1 Cup Nut Milk of Your
Choosing
1 tsp Chia Seeds
1 Tbsp Pure Maple Syrup
1/2 tsp Vanilla Extract

PREP
5 MINS

SERVES
ONE

1. In a sealable jar or container, add all ingredients, shake it or stir to combine ingredients.
2. Then add in any of the additional recipes on the following pages. Your options are endless!
3. Let sit in fridge overnight or for at least 8 hours. Enjoy in the morning cold, or microwave to have hot cereal.

CHUNKY MONKEY OVERNIGHT OATS PARFAIT

1 Tbsp Peanut Butter Powder
1/2 Tbsp Cacao Nibs (or dark chocolate chips if you want it to be more decadent)
1/2 Tbsp Shredded, Unsweetened Coconut

TOPPINGS:
1 Banana
Extra Cacao Nibs, Coconut, and Creamy Peanut Butter

PREP
10 MINS

SERVES
1

INSTRUCTIONS

1. Add to the Overnight Oat base (page 28) the Peanut Powder, cacao nibs and the shredded coconut. Mix and place in a mason jar overnight.
2. In the A.M. make a parfait layering the oat mixture, then the banana slices, then extra coconut, cacao, and a drizzle of peanut butter, oats, banana, coconut, cacao, PB, oats, banana etc. you get the idea.
3. Or if you are feeling less artsy and more groggy in the A.M. just dump the oats in a bowl and plop the toppings over top and eat up!

APPLE PIE OVERNIGHT OATS PARFAIT

1 Apple, peeled and chopped
1 tsp Cinnamon
1 Tbsp Pure Maple Syrup

1 Tbsp Water
Handful of Pecans, chopped

PREP
10 MINS

SERVES
1

INSTRUCTIONS

1. Make the overnight oats base recipe (page 28) and place in the fridge overnight.
2. In the morning, add the apples to a small saucepan along with the cinnamon, syrup, and water and bring to a boil.
3. Reduce to a simmer and cook until mixture begins to thicken (about 5 minutes).
4. Remove from heat and layer your overnight oats and filling into a parfait, or simply spoon the oats into bowls and top with filling.
5. Sprinkle with pecans and enjoy!

STRAWBERRIES & CREAM OVERNIGHT OATS PARFAIT

5 Strawberries, rinsed
and chopped
Strawberry Chia Jam
(page 133)
Coconut Whipped
Cream (page 162)

PREP
5 MINS

SERVES
ONE

1. Add the chopped strawberries to the Overnight Oat base recipe (page 28). Mix and place in the fridge in a jar overnight.
2. Prepare the strawberry chia jam and Coconut Whipped Cream.
3. In the morning take out your overnight oats, jam and whipped cream.
4. In a clean jar or dish of your choosing, layer everything like a parfait. A couple spoonfuls of oats, then jam, then cream, oats, jam, cream etc.

CHOCOLATE BROWNIE RAWNOLA

6 Medjool Dates, pitted
2 Tbsp Cacao Powder
1 Cup Oats

PREP
5 MINS

SERVES
ONE

1. Place all ingredients into a food processor or high speed blender.
2. Pulse (on and off, on and off) to bring ingredients all together.
3. You'll be left with a crumbly texture looking like granola.
4. Store in an air tight container in the fridge for up to 1 week.
5. You can enjoy your rawnola as a cereal just by pouring some nut milk over it or even mash it together with milk and enjoy it as a brownie dough!

CHOCOLATE PEANUT BUTTER OATMEAL

PREP
10 MINS

COOK
5 MINS

SERVES
ONE

INGREDIENTS

1/2 Cup Oats
1 Cup water
2-3 Pinches of Sea Salt
1/2 Banana
1/4 tsp Cinnamon

TOPPINGS:
1/2 Banana, sliced
1-2 Tbsp Dark, Dairy Free
Chocolate Chips
1/2 Cup of Chocolate
Brownie Rawnola (recipe
found on page 31)
1/4 Cup Nut Milk of Choice

CHOCOLATE SAUCE:
1 Tbsp Cacao Powder
1 Tbsp Pure Maple Syrup

PEANUT SAUCE:
2 Tbsp Powdered Peanut
Butter
2 Tbsp Water

INSTRUCTIONS

1. Over Medium heat, add the oats, water and 1 pinch of salt. Stir and cook until you have an oatmeal consistency of your liking.
2. Mash 1/2 of your banana with a fork into a puree then add to your oats. Add your cinnamon and stir together.
3. Pour the oatmeal into your serving bowl and start to add your toppings.
4. Sprinkle the chocolate chips over top to get all melty.
5. Add the rawnola on top and pour the milk over the rawnola – this is a step that I feel is a must!
6. To make the last of your toppings, starting with the chocolate sauce, in a small bowl combine the cacao and maple syrup and stir with a fork or small whisk. Stir stir stir. This may take a while and might seem like it won't come together, but trust me it will and it will be SO worth it!
7. Do the same for the peanut sauce. This will come together a lot easier.
8. Pour both sauces over the top of your oatmeal creation and simple enjoy!

BANANA PANCAKES

2 Medium Ripe Bananas
3/4 Cups Nut Milk of
Your Choosing
1 Cup Rolled Oats
1 1/2 tsp Baking Powder
1/4 tsp Sea Salt

PREP
10 MINS

COOK
15 MINS

SERVES
2

1. In a blender, add bananas and almond milk. Blend until smooth.
2. Next add oats, baking powder, and salt into the blender; blend again until batter is well-combined. Set aside for 5 minutes to thicken up.
4. Cook pancakes on a nonstick griddle or pan, well coated with cooking spray. Start on a low heat and gradually bring up to medium low. 325 degrees is perfect for a griddle.
5. Top pancake with berries, nut butter, pure maple syrup etc.

CINNAMON FRENCH TOAST

1 Cup Nut Milk of Choice
1 Tbsp Ground Flax Seeds
1 tsp Vanilla Extract
1/2 tsp Cinnamon
1/4 tsp All Apice
1 Tbsp Coconut Oil
4-6 slices of Hearty Bread
(page 93)

PREP
10 MINS

COOK
15 MINS

SERVES
4-6

1. In a large bowl, add the milk, flax meal, vanilla, cinnamon and all spice, whisk, and set aside while you heat up your griddle or pan.
2. Heat the coconut oil on a griddle or pan over medium-low heat.
3. One side at a time, dip bread into the batter, covering all corners (no gaps).
4. Place slices on the griddle and cook for 5 minutes on each side, or until golden-brown.
5. Drizzle french toast with maple syrup or nut butter and top with fresh fruit.

PRETTY 'N' PINK PITAYA BOWL

1 Pack Frozen
Dragonfruit or 2 Tbsp
Dragonfruit Powder
1 Frozen Banana
1/2 Cup Frozen Mango
1/2 Cup Frozen
Strawberries
1/4 Cup Nut Milk of
Choice

PREP
5 MINS

SERVES
ONE

1. Place all ingredients into a high speed blender.
2. Blend until smooth like soft serve ice cream.
3. Pour out into a bowl and place fresh fruit and any toppings of your choosing on top. (See suggested toppings on page 23)

Tip: For a lower sugar version,
just replace 1 banana with
1 cup of frozen cauliflower

MORNING GLOW SMOOTHIE BOWL

1 Frozen Banana
1/2 Cup Frozen Mango
1 Cup Frozen
Cauliflower
1/4 Cup Fresh Zucchini
2 Large Handfuls of
Spinach
2 Tbsp Vanilla Plant-
Based Protein Powder
1/2 tsp Spirulina
Powder (optional)
1 Tbsp Flax Seeds
8oz Coconut Water

PREP
5 MINS

SERVES
ONE

1. Place all ingredients into a high speed blender and blend until smooth.
2. Pour smoothie into a large bowl and top with any of the toppings listed on page 23.

BEST BAKED DONUTS

PREP
10 MINS

MAKES
6

2 Cups Medjool Dates, pitted
1/2 Cup Nut Milk
1 tsp Apple Cider Vinegar
1 tsp Vanilla Extract
1 1/2 tsp Baking Powder

1 tsp Baking Soda
3/4 Cup Oat Flour
1/2 Cup Almond Flour
1 Tbsp Arrowroot Flour
Pinch of Sea Salt

INSTRUCTIONS

1. Add the dates, nut milk, vinegar, and vanilla to a food processor and blend until smooth.
2. To a large bowl, mix together the remaining dry ingredients.
3. Add the date mixture to the dry and mix with a spatula until you have a dough.
4. Into a donut pan, evenly disperse the batter and bake in the oven for 10 minutes at 350F.
5. Let cool completely in the pan then frost with any frosting you like. I highly recommend the Cashew Frosting (page 151), Chocolate Frosting (page 151), or the chocolate ganache (page 162)
6. *If you do not have a donut pan, you could also roll into balls to make donut holes!

BLUEBERRY DONUT

1/2 Cup Fresh or Frozen Blueberries

1. For a blueberry variation of the donut above: after step 3, place everything in a mixing bowl and gently fold in the blueberries before baking.

CHOCOLATE DONUT

1/2 Cup Cocoa Powder
2 Tbsp Nut Milk

1. For a chocolate variation of the donut above: after step 2, add in the cocoa powder and additional milk with everything, blend and bake!

entree's

SPAGHETTI SQUASH ALFREDO BAKE

PREP
10 MINS

COOK
1 HOUR

SERVES
4-6

INGREDIENTS

1 Large Spaghetti Squash, cut lengthwise with seeds removed
1/2 Bell Pepper, diced
1 Cup Broccoli Florets, chopped into small pieces
1 Cup Button Mushrooms, sliced
1/2 Cup Frozen Peas
5 Strips of Prepared Baked Bacon Tempeh (page 102)
1 Garlic Clove, minced
2 Tbsp Fresh Basil, chopped
Prepared Alfredo Sauce (page 130)

INSTRUCTIONS

1. Line a baking sheet with parchment paper and place the spaghetti squash halves on the paper cut side down and bake for 40 minutes at 400°F.
2. After the squash has cooled enough to handle, use a fork to scoop out the strands of squash and place into a mixing bowl.
3. Add the bell pepper, broccoli, mushrooms, peas, tempeh, garlic and basil to the same bowl and stir to combine it with the squash then pour into a baking dish.
4. Pour the prepared alfredo sauce over everything in the baking dish, spread out evenly and bake for 20 minutes at 350°F.

INSTANT POT MUSHROOM BUTTERNUT RISOTTO

PREP
10 MINS

COOK
1 HOUR

SERVES
4-6

INGREDIENTS

1/2 Yellow Onion, chopped
3 Cloves of Garlic, minced
1 Red Bell Pepper, diced
2 Cups Butternut Squash, cubed
1 1/2 Cups of Arborio Rice
3 1/2 Cups of Vegetable Broth
1 Cup Shiitake Mushrooms, sliced
1 Cup Asparagus, roughly chopped
1 1/2 tsp Salt
1/2 tsp Black Pepper
1/2 tsp Coriander
1/2 tsp Oregano
1/2 Cup Frozen Peas
2 Tbsp Nutritional Yeast

INSTRUCTIONS

1. Using an instant pot, add your onion, garlic, pepper, and squash together with a splash of water and turn on the sauté feature, stir until soft and slightly brown (about 3 minutes)
2. Add the rice to the pot, and stir.
3. Add the remaining ingredients (except for the peas and nutritional yeast) into the pot and stir.
4. Close the lid and seal the pressure lid.
5. Press "manual" and reduce the time to 10 minutes
6. When the timer goes off, turn your instant pot off and let sit for 10-15 minutes before releasing the pressure to open.
7. Stir in your peas and nutritional yeast and serve!

MAC 'N' CHEESE

PREP
10 MINS

COOK
15 MINS

SERVES
4-6

INGREDIENTS

1 Cup Soaked Cashews
1 Cup Water
¼ Cup Nutritional Yeast
1 Tbsp Hemp Heart Seeds
1 Tbsp Tomato Paste
1 Tbsp Apple Cider Vinegar
1 tsp Sea Salt
1 Garlic Clove
2 tsp Onion Powder
1 1/2 tsp Dijon Mustard

Macaroni Noodles (I like to use gluten free quinoa noodles)

INSTRUCTIONS

1. Fill a large pot with water 2/3 of the way and bring to a boil.
2. Add in your noodles and reduce boil to medium heat. Allow to cook 7-10 minutes to your liking.
3. While the noodles are cookin', drain and rinse the soaked cashews and place in a blender or food processor along with other ingredients (including water).
4. Once noodles are al dente or to your liking, drain and place back in pot.
5. Pour your sauce over the pasta and mix.
6. Store any left-over sauce in the fridge for up to a week. The sauce is great mixed with marinara for a creamier pasta sauce too!

Tip: Use Zucchini Noodles or
Kelp Noodles in place of
the macaroni for a lighter option!

TBLT (TEMPEH BACON LETTUCE TOMATO) SANDWICH

3-4 Slices of prepared
Tempeh Bacon (page
102)
2 Slices of Hearty
Bread (page 93) or
any bread
2-3 Slices of Tomato
3-4 large leaves of
lettuce
2-3 Tbsp prepared
Avocado Aioli (page
130)

PREP
5 MINS

SERVES
ONE

1. Toast bread then spread the aioli on each slice. Add your
   lettuce, tomato and tempeh on top of each other over the
   bread.
2. Slice in half and enjoy!

VEGGIE POWERHOUSE SANDWICH

2 Slices Hearty Bread
(page 93)
2-3 Tbsp Dill Pickle
Ranch Hummus
(page 129)
6 Slices of Cucumber
1/4 Red Pepper, thinly
sliced
1/4 Avocado, sliced
1/4 Cup Carrots, shredded
2-3 Lettuce Leaves

PREP
5 MINS

SERVES
ONE

1. Spread your hummus of choice on both slices of bread.
2. Assemble a tower of veggies on top of one slice of bread.
3. Place your other piece of bread on top of your veggies, slice and enjoy!

TOMATO MOZZARELLA MELT

PREP
5 MINS

SERVES
ONE

2 Slices of Hearty Bread
(page 93) or any bread
2-3 Slices of Tomato
1 Tbsp of Fresh Basil,
chopped
2 Tbsp Mozzarella (page
131)
2 Tbsp Prepared
Avocado Aioli (page 130)
1/2 Tbsp Coconut Oil

1. To assemble your sandwich, spread the aioli on one slice of
   bread, on the other slice, spread the mozzarella. Then add
   the tomato and basil on top of the mozzarella.
2. Heat a skillet or pan on the stove to medium heat and add
   the coconut oil to the pan.
3. Place the sandwich on the pan and let cook on one side for 1
   minute (or until golden brown, then flip and cook another
   minute on the other side.
4. Slice and enjoy!

PESTO ZUCCHINI PASTA

2-3 Large Zucchini's, spriralized
1 Batch Prepared Pesto Sauce (page 127)
1/2 Cup Sun-dried Tomatoes, chopped
2 Tbsp Pine Nuts

PREP
10 MINS

COOK
10 MINS

SERVES
3-4

1. Start by spiralizing your zucchini's. If you do not have a spiralizer, you can use a potato peeler to make thick ribbons for your noodles.
2. In a large pan over medium heat, sauté your zucchini noodles for 1-2 minutes until they turn a brighter green and get a little bit softer.
3. In the same pan, add the pesto sauce and sun-dried tomatoes, stir everything together.
4. To serve, sprinkle the pine nuts on top and enjoy.

SWEET POTATO CHICKPEA CHEESEBURGER

PREP
20 MINS

COOK
25 MINS

SERVES
4

INGREDIENTS

BURGER PATTY:
1 Cup Cooked Mashed Sweet
Potato
1/2 Cup Cooked Quinoa
1 (15 oz) Can Chickpeas
1 tsp Chili Powder
1/4 tsp Smoked Paprika
1/2 tsp Oregano
1/2 tsp Garlic Powder
1/2 tsp Onion Powder
1/2 tsp Sea Salt

TOPPINGS:
1 Yellow Onion, sliced
1/2 Cup Button Mushrooms,
sliced
1 Garlic Clove, chopped
1/2-3/4 Cup Vegetable Broth
Sea Salt and Pepper to Taste
2 Tbsp Avocado Aioli (page
130)
2-3 Tbsp of Prepared
Mozzarella Cheese (page 131)
Hearty Bread (page 93) or any
hamburger bun you like

INSTRUCTIONS

1. Place all burger patty ingredients into a food processor and blend until everything is broken down and combined.
2. Separate mixture into 4 sections, pack those sections together with your hands to form a patty.
3. Place the patty's on a baking sheet lined with parchment paper and bake for 45 minutes at 400F, flipping the patty's half way through.
4. Place the onions, mushrooms, and garlic into a pan with just a 1/4 cup of the broth and bring to a simmer on the stove top. Sprinkle with salt and pepper. Once the broth has evaporated, place another 1/4 cup into the pan and repeat this process until your onions are yellow and translucent.
5. Place a patty onto 1 slice of bread and spread the aioli on the other slice. Top the burger with the Mozzarella and a large scoop of onions and mushrooms.
6. Add any additional toppings you like to the burger and serve.

ALFREDO MARGHERITA PIZZA

PREP
10 MINS

COOK
25 MINS

SERVES
2-4

INGREDIENTS

Quinoa Lentil Pizza Crust (page 109)
1/2 Cup Alfredo Sauce (page 130)
1 Batch Mozzarella Cheese (page 131)
3 Roma Tomatoes, diced
3 Tbsp Fresh Basil, chopped
1 tsp Balsamic Vinegar
1/4 tsp Sea Salt
Fresh Ground Pepper to Taste
1 tsp Dried Oregano

INSTRUCTIONS

1. While your crust is baking, prepare the bruschetta by combining the diced tomatoes, fresh basil, vinegar, salt, and pepper in a small bowl.

2. Spread the Alfredo Sauce onto the crust and spread evenly with a spatula or spoon.

3. Top with dollops of mozzarella cheese and bruschetta.

4. Sprinkle the dried oregano over everything and bake 10 minutes more at 425F.

5. Slice and serve!

BBQ CHICKPEA PIZZA

PREP
10 MINS

COOK
25 MINS

SERVES
2-4

INGREDIENTS

Quinoa Lentil Pizza Crust
(page 109)
1/2 Cup BBQ Sauce
(page 132)
1 Batch Mozzarella Cheese
(page 131)
1/2 Batch Prepared BBQ
Chickpeas (page 98)
1/4 Cup Red Onion, sliced
1/4 Cup Red Pepper
15 Pickled Jalapeños
2 Tbsp fresh Cilantro

INSTRUCTIONS

1. After your crust has been baked, spread the BBQ Sauce evenly onto the crust.
2. Top with dollops of mozzarella cheese and sprinkle the remaining ingredients as you like.
3. Bake 10 minutes more at 425F.
4. Slice and serve!

HOMEMADE MARINARA

PREP
10 MINS

COOK
35 MINS

SERVES
4

INGREDIENTS

1 Yellow Onion, Diced
2 Garlic Cloves, minced
2 28-oz Cans Diced
Tomatoes
3 Tbsp Tomato Paste
1 tsp Dried Oregano
1/4 tsp Marjoram
1 Tbsp Pure Maple Syrup
1 tsp Sea Salt
1/4 tsp Red Pepper Flakes
1/2 Cup Fresh Basil, chopped

INSTRUCTIONS

1. Heat a large pot over medium heat and add a few tbsp. of water along with the onions and garlic. Sauté until soft. Then add tomatoes, tomato paste, oregano, syrup, salt, and pepper flakes.
2. Bring to a simmer over medium heat. Then reduce heat to low and leave uncovered for 30 minutes, stirring occasionally.
3. Then add basil, stir, and cook for 5 more minutes.
4. Add additional water if sauce is too thick to your liking.

Tip: This makes for a
fantastic
pizza sauce too!

MEAT-LESS BALLS

PREP
10 MINS

COOK
20 MINS

MAKES
15

INGREDIENTS

1 15oz Can of Kidney or
Black Beans
1 Clove Garlic, minced
1/2 Yellow Onion, diced
1 tsp Dried Basil
1 tsp Dried Oregano
1 Tbsp Tomato Paste
1 tsp Tamari or Liquid Aminos
1/4 Cup + 2 Tbsp Chickpea
Flour
2 Tbsp Nutritional Yeast
1/2 tsp Salt
Black Pepper to Taste

INSTRUCTIONS

1. In a pan, cook the onion in a few tbsp. of water until translucent, then add in the garlic for just 30 seconds and remove from heat.
2. While that cooks, crack open your can of beans, drain and rinse them.
3. In a large bowl, with a potato masher or a fork, start mashing up your beans.
4. Add your cooked onions and garlic to the beans along with all the other ingredients.
5. Mash and mix everything together with a spatula or with your best tools... your hands!
6. Roll heaping tablespoons of your mixture together into balls and place on a baking sheet lined with parchment paper.
7. Bake at 400 F for 20 minutes.

SPAGHETTI & MEAT-LESS BALLS

PREP
10 MINS

COOK
10 MINS

SERVES
4

INGREDIENTS

2-3 Large Zucchini's, spriralized (or you can use whatever noodles you like)
1 Batch Prepared Homemade Marinara Sauce (page 58)
1 Batch Prepared Meatless Balls (page 59)

Optional: Hemp Parmesan (page 103) or Mozzarella (page 131) to top your spaghetti

INSTRUCTIONS

1. Start by spiralizing your zucchini's. If you do not have a spiralizer, you can use a potato peeler to make thick ribbons for your noodles. And if you would rather use a regular pasta noodle, feel free to cook that instead.
2. In a large pan over medium heat, saute your zucchini noodles for 1-2 minutes until they turn a brighter green and get a bit softer.
3. Place your noodles on a serving plate then add a large scoop or two of the marinara sauce on top with a few meatless balls.
4. Sprinkle with some parmesan or mozzarella if you would like and enjoy!

TEMPEH TACOS

PREP
10 MINS

COOK
10 MINS

SERVES
4

INGREDIENTS

TACO SEASONING:
1 Tbsp Chili Powder
1/4 tsp Garlic Powder
1/4 tsp Onion Powder
1/4 tsp Dried Oregano
1/2 tsp Paprika
1 1/2 tsp Ground Cumin
1 tsp Salt
1 tsp Black Pepper

TACOS:
1 oz Package of Gluten Free
Tempeh, roughly chopped
Whole Butter Lettuce Leaves
Corn Tortillas
1 Avocado, cubed
Juice from 1 Lime
Nacho Cheese (page 132)
Salsa (page 126)

INSTRUCTIONS

1. To prepare the taco "meat" combine the spices for the taco seasoning in a small bowl.
2. Add the tempeh into a large sauté pan on the stove and start to cook in 2 Tbsp of water at medium-high heat.
3. Stir in the taco seasoning and add another few Tbsp of water.
4. Continue to stir and break up the tempeh to little crumbles. When you see all the water evaporate, add another few Tbsp. Use as much water as needed to keep your pan from drying.
5. Continue to stir and cook for 3 minutes and remove from heat.
6. To assemble your tacos, take a corn tortilla and place a few leaves of butter lettuce on top, then a few spoonfuls of taco meat, avocado, salsa and nacho cheese. Squeeze a bit of lime juice on top and enjoy!
7. If you would like to omit the corn tortillas you can always make lettuce wraps with the butter lettuce instead.

PUMPKIN CURRY

PREP
10 MINS

COOK
30 MINS

SERVES
4

INGREDIENTS

1 Yellow Onion, roughly
chopped
2 Garlic Cloves, minced
1 Cup Carrots, chopped
1 Can Diced Tomatoes
1 15-oz Can Pumpkin Puree
1 15-oz Can of Chickpeas,
drained and rinsed
1 Tbsp Curry Powder
1/2 tsp Ground Ginger
1/2 tsp Sea Salt
1/4 tsp Black Pepper
1/4 tsp Ground Turmeric
1/4 tsp Ground Cinnamon
1/8 tsp Ground Cayenne
1 13.5-oz Can Coconut Milk
(make sure to use full-fat)

INSTRUCTIONS

1. In a large wok (or pot) over medium heat,
   sauté the onion in 1 Tbsp of water. Cook
   until soft then add the garlic and cook for
   30 seconds more.
2. Add the carrots and tomatoes. Add a few
   more Tbsp of water when needed to keep
   from sticking. Cook until the carrots are
   tender.
3. Add the pumpkin, chickpeas, curry, ginger,
   salt, pepper, turmeric, cinnamon, and
   cayenne to the pot and stir to combine.
4. Place the coconut milk into the pot and stir.
5. Bring everything to a boil then reduce to a
   simmer. Cover for 15 minutes.
6. Serve your curry over prepared quinoa, rice or
   white potatoes and enjoy!

FULLY LOADED NACHOS

PREP
10 MINS

COOK
8 MINS

SERVES
2-3

INGREDIENTS

1/2 Batch Prepared Nacho
Cheese (page 132)
1 Batch Prepared Salsa
(page 126)
8 Corn Tortillas
1 Cup Canned Refried Beans
(pinto or black)
1/2 Cup Frozen Corn, thawed
20 Black Olives, sliced
10 Pickled Jalapenos

INSTRUCTIONS

1. Cut your corn tortillas into quarters (making little triangles) and place on a baking sheet. Bake for 6-8 minutes at 425F until tortillas are crispy all the way around.
2. Heat the refried beans in a sauce pan just until warm.
3. Scoop a spoonful of beans on top of each chip, then pour your nacho cheese over the chips (as much as you desire).
4. Sprinkle and dollop the remaining ingredients over the chips as you like.
5. You may need to make a few layers of chips on top of the other depending on how large your serving plate is.
6. Have fun with it and make it how you like!

SOUP
&
SALAD

BBQ NOURISH BOWL

PREP
10 MINS

SERVES
ONE

INGREDIENTS

3/4 Cup BBQ Chickpeas
Recipe (page 98)
1/2 Cup Cooked Quinoa
4 Cup Fresh Lettuce (any
variety)
1/4 Cup Red Bell Pepper
1/4 Cup Shredded Carrots
1/2 Cup Cherry Tomatoes,
halved
1/2 Cup Corn (cooked from a
cob, or thawed from frozen)
1/2 Avocado, cubed
1 Green Onion, diced
2 Tbsp Barbeque Sauce (page
132)
2-3 Tbsp Creamy Ranch
Dressing (page 129)

INSTRUCTIONS

1. To assemble the bowl, place all ingredients
   into a large serving bowl and toss together.
2. Add in the Creamy Ranch Dressing and
   BBQ Sauce and toss once more.

SWEET POTATO NOURISH BOWL

PREP
10 MINS

COOK
20 MINS

SERVES
ONE

INGREDIENTS

SWEET POTATO:
1 Large Sweet Potato
1 tsp Chili Powder
Salt + Pepper

ASSEMBLE THE BOWL:
Sweet Potato (from above)
3/4 Cup Canned Black
Beans, drained and rinsed
1/2 Cup Cooked Quinoa
3-4 Cup Fresh Green Lettuce
(any variety)
1/2 Avocado, cubed
2-3 Tbsp Avocado-Cilantro
Dressing (page 134)

INSTRUCTIONS

1. To make the Sweet Potato (can do this night before), preheat the oven to 425F.
2. Peel and chop the sweet potato in small, bite-sized pieces. Toss potato with chili powder and sprinkle with salt and pepper, tossing to combine.
3. Roast sweet potato for 20 minutes until tender, tossing half way through.
1. To assemble the bowl, place all ingredients into a large serving bowl and toss together with the Avocado-Cilantro Dressing.

THAI CHICKPEA NOURISH BOWL

PREP
10 MINS

COOK
25 MINS

SERVES
ONE

INGREDIENTS

CHICKPEAS:
3/4 Cup Canned Chickpeas
1 tsp Fresh Lemon Juice
1/4 tsp Sea Salt
1/4 tsp Garlic Powder
1/2 tsp Onion Powder
1/2 tsp Curry Powder

ASSEMLE THE BOWL:
Baked Chickpeas (from above)
1/2 Cup Cooked Quinoa
2 Cups Spring Greens
1/4 Cup Purple Cabbage
2 Tbsp Cilantro (more if you love cilantro)
1/4 Cup Red Bell Pepper
1/4 Cup Shredded Carrots
2 Tbsp Red Onion, chopped
1 Green Onion, sliced
1/2 Avocado, cubed
1 Tbsp Almonds, chopped
2-3 Tbsp Almond-Tahini Dressing (page 134)

INSTRUCTIONS

1. To make the chickpeas, preheat your oven to 400F. Drain, rinse and dry chickpeas with a towel.
2. Spread out the peas on a baking sheet with parchment paper. Roast for 20-25 minutes, until chickpeas are crunchy.
3. Remove from oven and toss chickpeas with the lemon salt and spices.
4. To assemble the bowl, place all ingredients into a large serving bowl and toss together with the Almond-Tahini Dressing.
5. *Optional: If you want a peanuty thai bowl, just replace the almond butter in the dressing with peanut butter. And use chopped peanuts instead of almonds.

POTATO CORN CHOWDER

PREP
10 MINS

COOK
15-30 MINS

SERVES
4-6

INGREDIENTS

6 Red Potatoes, diced
2 Cups Frozen or Fresh Corn
1 Yellow Onion, diced
1 Medium Carrot, diced
1/2 Red Pepper, chopped
3 Cups Vegetable Broth
1 Cup Nut Milk of Choice
3 Tbsp Arrowroot Flour
1 tsp Sea Salt
2 Tbsp Nutritional Yeast
Pepper to Taste

INSTRUCTIONS

INSTANT POT:
1. With the sauté function, sauté the onions with 3 Tbsp of water until soft.
2. Add the diced potatoes, carrots, corn, pepper, salt, flour and yeast to the pot and stir.
3. Add the vegetable broth and milk and stir again.
4. Turn on the "soup" feature and close the lid and steam valve. Set for 15 minutes.
5. When Instant Pot is finished, carefully release the steam valve and then the lid when steam is gone.
6. Give the soup a taste and add extra salt and pepper to your liking.

STOVE TOP:
1. Start by sautéing the onions with 3 Tbsp of water until soft.
2. Add the diced potatoes, carrots, corn, pepper, salt, flour and yeast to the pot and stir.
3. Add the vegetable broth and milk and stir again.
4. Bring to a boil then to a simmer and cover for 30 minutes.
5. Give the soup a taste and add extra salt and pepper to your liking.

KALE CAESAR SALAD

PREP
10 MINS

SERVES
4

INGREDIENTS

4 Cups Fresh Kale, chopped
4 Cups Romaine Lettuce, chopped
5 Strips Prepared Baked Tempeh Bacon (page 102)
1 Batch Prepared Caesar Dressing (page 134)
Prepared Garlic Bread Chickpeas (page 99)
1/2 Cup Prepared Hemp Parmesan (page 103)

INSTRUCTIONS

1. In a large bowl, combine the kale and romaine. Toss with the dressing (start with pouring in half the batch of dressing and add more to your liking)
2. Crumble the tempeh bacon into the salad, sprinkle in the parmesan and chickpeas and toss everything together once more.

QUINOA CHILI

PREP
10 MINS

COOK
15-30 MINS

SERVES
4-6

INGREDIENTS

2 1/2 Cups Vegetable Broth
1/2 Cup Uncooked Quinoa
15-oz Can Black Beans
15-oz Can Diced Tomatoes
1/2 Chopped Bell Pepper
1 Carrot, shredded
1/2 Onion, chopped
2 Cloves Garlic, minced
2 tsp Chili Powder
1/4 tsp Cayenne Pepper
1 1/2 tsp Sea Salt
1 tsp Ground Black Pepper
1 tsp Ground Cumin
1 tsp Oregano
1/2 Cup Frozen Corn Kernels

INSTRUCTIONS

INSTANT POT:
1. Place all ingredients in an instant pot, stir and cover with lid.
2. Press the "soup" button and set the time to 15 minutes.

STOVE TOP:
1. To cook on the stove top, place all the ingredients in a large pot and bring to a boil. Set to simmer for 30 minutes and stir every 15 minutes.
2. Yep, that simple! Enjoy!

PESTO TOMATO CHICKPEA SALAD

2 Cups Cherry
Tomatoes, halved
15-oz Can
Chickpeas, drained and
rinsed
2 Cup Spinach, chopped
1 Cup Cucumber, sliced
1/4 tsp Sea Salt
1/2 Batch of Pesto Sauce
(page 127)
1/4 Cup Pine Nuts or
Almonds, chopped

PREP   SERVES

5 MINS   4

1. Chop up all fresh veggies and place into a large mixing
   bowl and toss with 1/4 tsp sea salt.
2. Make a batch of the Pesto sauce.
3. Mix in your pesto with the veggies.
4. Serve with chopped pine nuts or almonds on top

CREAMY CABBAGE SLAW

1 Head of Napa Cabbage,
chopped
1 Cup Red Cabbage,
chopped
1/2 Cup Carrots, shredded
2 Green Onions, chopped
1 Cup Raw Peas (or
thawed from frozen)
3 Tbsp Cilantro, chopped
Juice of 1/2 a Lime
1 Batch of Almond-Tahini
Dressing
(page 134)

2 Tbsp Cashews or
Almonds, chopped

PREP
10 MINS

SERVES
4

1. Chop up all your veggies and place into the biggest bowl in your kitchen.
2. Pour the Almond-Tahini Dressing over your ingredients and toss it all around!
3. Cover your bowl with a fitted lid or plastic wrap and let sit for 4-24 hours. The longer it marinates, the tastier it will be!
4. Top with chopped nuts of your choosing when ready to serve!

BROCCOLI CHEESE SOUP

PREP
15 MINS

COOK
8-15 MINS

SERVES
3-4

INGREDIENTS

1 Batch Prepared Cheese
Sauce from the Mac 'N'
Cheese recipe on page 47
1 Yellow Onion, chopped
2 Cloves Garlic, minced
1/2 tsp Sea Salt
4 CupS Broccoli
Florets, roughly chopped
1 Cup Red Potatoes
4 Cups Vegetable Broth

INSTRUCTIONS

INSTANT POT:
1. With the sauté function, sauté the onions with 3 Tbsp of water until soft.
2. Stir in the garlic and cook for 1 minute. Add broccoli florets, potatoes, and vegetable broth and bring to a boil and let simmer for 5 minutes.
3. Place half the broccoli, potato and broth mixture into a high speed blender and pulse a few times leaving some of the chunks still in tact.
4. Return the blended mixture to the pot and pour in your prepared cheese sauce then turn on "manual" function and set for 8 minutes.
5. When Instant Pot is finished, carefully release the steam valve and then lid when steam is gone.

STOVE TOP:
1. Heat a large saucepan with a few Tbsp of water over medium-high heat. Add onion and saute until soft.
2. Stir in the garlic and cook for another minute. Add in your broccoli florets, potatoes, and vegetable broth and bring to a boil. Reduce heat to simmer for 5 minutes until broccoli is tender.
3. Place half the broccoli, potato and broth mixture into a high speed blender and pulse a few times leaving some of the chunks still in tact.
4. Return the blended mixture to the saucepan and pour in your prepared cheese sauce and cook everything together, cover for another 10 minutes. Stirring every few minutes.

WILD RICE SOUP

PREP
10 MINS

COOK
30 MINS

SERVES
4-6

INGREDIENTS

1/2 Cup Dry Wild Rice
6 Red Potatoes, diced
1 Yellow Onion, diced
1 Medium Carrot, diced
2 Celery Stalks, diced
3 Cups Vegetable Broth
1 Cup Nut Milk of Choice
3 Tbsp Arrowroot Flour
1 tsp Sea Salt
1 tsp Dried Thyme
2 Tbsp Nutritional Yeast
Pepper to Taste

INSTRUCTIONS

INSTANT POT:
1. With the sauté function, sauté the onions with 3 tbsp of water until soft.
2. Add the diced potatoes, carrots, salt, thyme, flour and yeast to the pot and stir.
3. Add the vegetable broth, milk, and wild rice and stir again.
4. Turn on the "soup" feature and close the lid and steam valve. Set for 30 minutes.
6. When Instant Pot is finished, carefully release the steam valve and then lid when steam is gone.
7. Give the soup a taste and add extra salt and pepper to your liking

STOVETOP:
1. Start by cooking your wild rice. Combine 1/2 Cup wild rice with 1 cup water in a pot on the stove. Bring to a boil then turn off the the burner and cover the pot. Let sit for 20 minutes.
2. In a large pot, saute the onions with 3 Tbsp of water until soft.
3. Add the diced potatoes, carrots, corn, salt, thyme, flour and yeast to the pot and stir.
4. Add the vegetable broth, milk, and wild rice (drain excess water from it) and stir again.
5. Bring to a boil then to a simmer and cover for 30 minutes.
6. Give the soup a taste and add extra salt and pepper to your liking.

TORTILLA SOUP

PREP
10 MINS

COOK
15-30 MINS

SERVES
4-6

INGREDIENTS

1 Yellow Onion, chopped
1/2 Bell Pepper
2 Jalapeno Peppers, deseeded and diced
5 Cloves Garlic, minced
1 28-oz Can Diced Tomatoes
3 Cups Vegetable Stock
2- 6 inch Corn Tortilla, cut into 1/2 inch Pieces
1 Tbsp Chili Powder
1 tsp Garlic Powder
2 tsp Ground Cumin
1/2 Cup Frozen Corn
1 19-oz Can Black Beans, rinsed and drained
2 tsp Sea Salt
Black Pepper to Taste

Top with Avocado, Cilantro and Crispy Corn Tortilla's (follow directions on page 67) for Garnish

INSTRUCTIONS

INSTANT POT:

1. Using the sauté function, add the onion, peppers and garlic into the pot and sauté with a a few Tbsp of water until soft.
2. Add the remaining ingredients to the pot, stir and turn on the "soup" function and close the lid and steam valve. Set for 15 minutes.
3. When Instant Pot is finished, carefully release the steam valve and then lid when steam is gone
4. Serve with some avocado, cilantro and crispy corn tortilla's.

STOVETOP:

1. Over medium-high heat place your chopped onion, peppers and garlic into a pot and sauté with a a few Tbsp of water until soft.
2. Add the remaining ingredients to the pot, stir and bring to a boil.
3. Bring to a simmer and cover with a lid for 30 minutes.
4. Serve with some avocado, cilantro and crispy corn tortilla's.

snacks
&
staples

HEARTY BREAD

PREP
1 HOUR

COOK
45 MINS

SLICES
12-14

INGREDIENTS

5 1/4 Cups Oat Flour
3 Tbsp Active Yeast
2 1/4 Cups Warm Water
1/4 Cup Unsweetened Apple Sauce
2 Tbsp Olive Oil
1/2 Cup Pure Maple Syrup
3/4 Cup Arrowroot Flour
3/4 Cup Chickpea Flour
1 Tbsp Xanthan Gum
1 1/2 tsp Sea Salt
6 Flax Eggs (6 Tbsp Ground Flax Seeds + 1 Cup + 2 Tbsp Water)

INSTRUCTIONS

1. In a small bowl combine the yeast and water and let sit for a few minutes.
2. In another small bowl, combine the 6 Tbsp flax seeds + 1 Cup & 2 Tbsp water to make the flax eggs. Let sit for a few minutes to thicken.
3. Add the remaining ingredients to a bowl of a stand mixer.
4. After both the yeast and flax mixtures have thickened, add those to the stand mixer bowl. Mix everything with a paddle attachment for 2-3 minutes.
5. Pour into a 9X5 bread pan and allow to sit for 45 minutes to rise.
6. After the 45 minutes, sprinkle the top with whole oats (optional step) and cut 2 slits at a diagonal across the top of the bread with a serrated knife. Bake for 45 minutes at 350F.
7. Allow to cool completely before slicing. It's hard to wait but letting it cool completely is a crucial step.

CRISPY FRENCH FRIES

PREP
10 MINS

COOK
30 MINS

SERVES
2-4

INGREDIENTS

4 Large Russet Potatoes
1 tsp of Sea Salt
1/2 tsp Paprika
1/2 tsp Garlic Powder
1/2 tsp Onion Powder
1/8 tsp of Cayenne
1/8 tsp Black Pepper
18 tsp Turmeric

INSTRUCTIONS

1. Rinse and scrub your potatoes then slice them into thin fry shapes and place in a large bowl.
2. Mix seasonings together and sprinkle over fries. Toss together in the bowl.
3. Arrange the potatoes in a single layer on a baking sheet lined with a Silpat (Silicone Mat).
4. Place the potatoes in the oven before preheating the oven.
5. Set the timer for 30 minutes and set oven at a temperature of 425F.
6. Using a tongs, remove each fry and enjoy with some BBQ Sauce (page 132), Ranch (page 135), or any sauce you like! They're dang good by themselves too!

CAULFLOWER BUFFALO & BBQ BITES

PREP
10 MINS

COOK
30 MINS

SERVES
2-3

INGREDIENTS

1 Head Cauliflower, cut into
bite-sized pieces
1/2 Cup Almond Flour
1/2 Cup Vegetable Broth
1/2 tsp Garlic
1/2 tsp Onion Powder
1/2 tsp Sea Salt
1/4 tsp Black Pepper

FOR THE BUFFALO BITES:
3/4 Cup Vegan Hot Sauce of
Your Choosing

FOR THE BBQ BITES:
3/4 Cup BBQ Sauce on
page 132

INSTRUCTIONS

1. In a large bowl, mix together the flour,
   broth, garlic, salt, and pepper.
2. Add the cauliflower pieces into the bowl,
   stir and flip them around until all are
   coated with the batter.
3. Place the cauliflower pieces on the
   parchment.
4. Bake at 350F for 30 minutes, or until the
   cauliflower is golden brown.
5. As soon as the cauliflower comes out of
   the oven, coat each with the hot sauce or
   BBQ sauce and serve immediately with
   some ranch. (page 135)

BARBEQUE CHICKPEAS

1 15-oz Can of
Chickpeas
1 tsp Pure Maple Syrup
1 tsp Smoked Paprika
1 tsp Chili Powder
1/2 tsp Garlic Powder
1/2 tsp Onion Powder
1/2 tsp Cumin
1/4 tsp Sea Salt

PREP
5 MINS

COOK
25 MINS

SERVES
2-3

1. Preheat your oven to 400F. Drain, rinse, and dry chickpeas with a towel.
2. Spread the chickpeas out on a baking sheet lined with parchment paper. Roast for 20-25 minutes, until chickpeas are crunchy.
3. Remove from oven and toss the peas in the maple syrup and spices.
4. Store in air tight container for up to 3 days.

GARLIC BREAD CHICKPEAS

1 15-oz Can of
Chickpeas
2 tsp Lemon Juice
1/4 tsp Sea Salt
1 tsp Garlic Powder
1 tsp Onion Powder

PREP
5 MINS

COOK
25 MINS

SERVES
2-3

1. Preheat your oven to 400F. Drain, rinse and dry chickpeas with a towel.
2. Spread the chickpeas out on a baking sheet lined with parchment paper. Roast for 20-25 minutes.
3. Remove from oven and toss the chickpeas in lemon juice, salt, garlic, and onion powder.
4. Store in air tight container for up to 3 days.

CHICK-PEA NUGGETS

PREP
10 MINS

COOK
15 MINS

MAKES
12

INGREDIENTS

1/2 Cup Chickpea
Breadcrumbs (or you can use
any gluten-free
breadcrumbs)
1/2 Cup Oat Flour
1 15-oz Can of Chickpeas 1/4
Cup Aquafaba (liquid from
chickpea can)
1 tsp Sea Salt
1/2 tsp Garlic Powder
1/2 tsp Onion Powder
Pinch Black Pepper
Pinch Cayenne Pepper

INSTRUCTIONS

1. Place the breadcrumbs on a baking sheet and bake for 5 minutes at 400F until they are golden brown.
2. Transfer crumbs to a bowl and let cool.
4. Drain the chickpeas over a bowl to save the liquid from the can. You'll only need 1/4 Cup of the liquid.
5. Place the chickpeas, salt, garlic, onion powder and pepper into a food processor and pulse (on, off, on, off) until you get a crumbly mixture.
6. Add the aquafaba and oat flour to the food processor with the chickpea mixture and pulse. You should be left with a big dough ball.
7. Shape the dough into 12 like-sized nuggets.
8. Roll each nugget in the breadcrumbs and place a baking sheet lined with parchment.
9. Bake nuggets for 15 minutes at 375F or until crispy.
10. Serve with BBQ Sauce (page 132) avocado aioli (page 130) or Creamy Ranch (page 135). So many dipping options!

BAKED TEMPEH BACON

1 8-oz Package
Gluten Free Tempeh
1/4 Cup Liquid Aminos
1 Tbsp Pure Maple
Syrup
1 Tbsp Liquid Smoke

PREP 5 MINS

COOK 25 MINS

SERVES 2-3

1. Slice tempeh into very thin strips.
2. Place Tempeh in a glass baking dish.
3. Combine liquid aminos, maple syrup, and liquid smoke together then pour over tempeh.
4. Marinade overnight in the fridge, or for at least an hour.
5. Place baking dish in the oven and bake for 20 minutes at 350F, flipping the tempeh half way through.
6. If you'd like it crispy, you can also fry up the bacon on the stove top like regular old bacon. You will have to use oil with this option.

HEMP PARMESAN CHEESE

1 Cup Hemp Heart
Seeds
1/4 Cup Nutritional
Yeast
1/4 tsp Pink Himalayan
Salt
1/2 tsp Garlic Powder

PREP
10 MINS

1. Add all ingredients to a food processor or blender and pulse (on and off, on and off) a few times until everything is mingling. Or just feel free to mix in a bowl if you don't have access to a machine.
2. Store in an air tight container in the fridge.

SALTED CARAMEL POPCORN

PREP
10 MINS

COOK
15 MINS

SERVES
2-3

INGREDIENTS

1/2 Cup Popcorn Kernels
2 Tbsp Coconut Oil
1/2 tsp Sea Salt
2 Tbsp Nut Milk of Choice
1/4 Cup + 2 Tbsp Pure Maple Syrup
2 Tbsp Coconut Sugar
1 tsp Vanilla
1/2 tsp Baking Soda

INSTRUCTIONS

1. Using a whirly pop, air popper, or whatever device you like to pop your corn in, pop the half cup of popcorn.

2. In a pot over medium high heat, add the oil, salt, milk, syrup, coconut sugar and vanilla; whisk to combine.

3. Allow this mixture to come to a boil, then add in the baking soda and stir for a minute longer. Reduce heat to low, whisking frequently at this point for 1 more minute.

4. Remove from the heat and pour over your prepared popcorn (in a large bowl). Toss the popcorn with a spatula quickly to evenly distribute onto your popped corn.

5. Spread the popcorn over a baking sheet lined with parchment paper.

6. Bake for 15 minutes at 325F. Remove from the oven and allow the popcorn to cool.

7. Enjoy immediately or stick in a fridge in an air tight container.

COOKIE DOUGH BLISS BALLS

1/2 Cup Almond Butter
1/4 Cup Vanilla Plant-Based Protein Powder
1/4 Cup Oat Flour
1/3 cup Almond Flour
1 Tbsp Pure Maple Syrup
1/2 tsp Vanilla Extract

1/4 tsp Almond Extract
1/4 tsp Cinnamon
Pinch of Sea Salt
3 Tbsp Nut Milk of Choice
2 Tbsp Dairy Free Dark Chocolate, chopped (or chips)

INSTRUCTIONS

1. In a bowl with a spatula, mix all the ingredients (except chocolate) until it forms a soft cookie dough. Add more milk if dough is too crumbly to roll out.
2. Stir in the chocolate chips and roll into 12 heaping tbsp balls.

CRANBERRY LEMON BLISS BALLS

1 1/2 Cups Almond Flour
1/2 Cup Oat Flour
2 Tbsp Pure Maple Syrup
Juice from 1 Lemon

Zest from 1 Lemon
1/4 Cup Mashed Ripe Banana
1/2 tsp Vanilla Extract
1/4 Cup Dried Cranberries

INSTRUCTIONS

1. Add the ingredients to a bowl and mix until you have a big chunk of dough.
2. Roll out heaping Tbsp of dough to form 12 balls.

CARROT CAKE BLISS BALLS

2 Carrots, grated (about 1/2 cup measured)
10 Pitted Dates
1/4 Cup Cashews
1/4 Cup Walnuts
3/4 Cups Oats
1/5 tsp Cardamom

1/4 tsp Cinnamon
Pinch of Sea Salt
1 Tbsp fresh Orange Juice
Fresh Zest from Half an Orange
1/3 Cup Shredded Coconut
2 Tbsp Walnuts, chopped

INSTRUCTIONS

1. Place everything (except the walnuts) in a food processor and blend until a dough forms and it all comes together.
2. Fold in the chopped walnuts with a spatula.
3. Roll into 12 heaping Tbsp balls then roll in coconut to finish off.

NO-BAKE PROTEIN BARS

PREP
10 MINS

SERVES
8

1 Cup Oat Flour
1 Cup Plant Based
Protein Powder (any
flavor your like)
1/2 Cup Nut Milk of
Choice
1/4 Cup Almond Butter
4 Medjool Dates, pitted
1 Tbsp Maca Powder
1 tsp Vanilla Extract
Pinch of Sea Salt

1. Combine everything in a food processor, pulsing until you have a crumbly dough. Test the dough to make sure it will stick together by pressing it with your fingers. Add a dash or two of milk if batter is too dry. The consistency will all depend on the protein powder you use and the size of the dates used.

2. Line a baking pan with parchment paper and pour in your dough pressing it out evenly with the back of a jar or flat drinking glass (this will help pack it in tight together).

3. Add a few cacao nibs or chocolate chips at this time if you like and press those in.

4. Refrigerate for at least 30 minutes before slicing into bars. Keep in an air tight container in the fridge or freezer.

QUINOA LENTIL PIZZA CRUST

PREP
10 MINS

COOK
25 MINS

SERVES
2-4

INGREDIENTS

3/4 Cup Dry Quinoa + 1/4
Cup Dry Red Lentils
(soaked overnight in 2 cups
water)
2 Tbsp Water
1 Tbsp Apple Cider Vinegar
1/2 Lemon, squeezed
1 Garlic Clove
1 tsp Italian Seasoning
Pinch Sea Salt and Pepper
1 Tbsp Nutritional Yeast

INSTRUCTIONS

1. Drain and rinse the soaked quinoa and lentils.
2. Preheat your oven to 425F.
3. Add the quinoa, 2 Tbsp of water, apple cider vinegar, lemon juice, garlic, nutritional yeast, seasoning, salt, and pepper to a high speed blender or food processor.
4. Blend for about 2 minutes or until mixture is smooth.
5. Pour batter out onto a pizza pan or baking sheet lined with parchment paper. With a spatula, spread the batter out into an even circle (you can make this as thick or thin as you'd like, the crust won't rise much)
6. Bake for 15 minutes or until golden and set.
7. Take out of the oven and top with whatever sauce and toppings you like.
8. Bake for another 10-12 minutes.
9. Cut and serve.

Drinks
&
Smoothie's

PUMPKIN MATCHA LATTE

1 Tsp Matcha Green Tea Powder
1/4 tsp Pumpkin Pie Spice
1/4 tsp Vanilla Powder (or extract)
1 tsp Pure Maple Syrup
Pinch or Two of Cinnamon
1/4 Cup Boiling Water
1 Tbsp Pumpkin Puree
9-oz Nut Milk of Choice

PREP
5 MINS

SERVES
ONE

1. In a mug of your choosing, place the Matcha, spice, vanilla, and cinnamon inside then pour in your boiling water and stir together.
2. To the boiled matcha mixture, add the pumpkin puree and stir until smooth.
3. Heat your almond milk in a pot and bring to a boil or a heat in a milk frother.
4. Pour warmed milk into your cup with all your other ingredients, stir and ENJOY!

MATCHA HOT CHOCOLATE

1 Tsp Matcha Green
Tea Powder
2 Tbsp Unsweetened
Cocoa Powder
1 tsp Vanilla Extract
1-2 Tbsp Pure Maple
Syrup
2 Pinch of Sea Salt
3 Tbsp Dark
Chocolate or Dairy
Free Chocolate Chips
1 Can Full Fat
Coconut Milk

PREP
2 MINS

COOK
5 MINS

SERVES
ONE

1. In a sauce pan, add all the ingredients and whisk on medium-high heat until the mixture comes to a boil.
2. If you would like some extra frothiness, add the hot chocolate to a blender and give it a quick blend. (this is an optional step)
3. Pour into your favorite mug and enjoy!

ICED GOLDEN LATTE

PREP
5 MINS

SERVES
ONE

INGREDIENTS

2 Cups Nut Milk of Choice
2 Tbsp Pure Maple Syrup (or
sweetener of choice)
1 tsp Turmeric Powder
1/4 tsp Cinnamon
1 Fingernail Slice of Fresh
Ginger (size of pinky
fingernail)
Pinch of Black Pepper
1/4 tsp Powdered Vanilla or
Extract

INSTRUCTIONS

1. Place all your ingredients into a blender and
   blend.
2. Pour over a tall glass of ice and enjoy.
3. If you would like to make a hot latte, just
   heat up the milk before blending.

PEAR-GINGER GREEN SMOOTHIE

1/2 Cup Nut Milk

2 Big Handfuls of Spinach

1 Pear, chopped

1/2 Frozen Banana

4 Ice Cubes

1/2 Inch Piece of Ginger, grated

1/4 tsp Ground Cinnamon

1/2 tsp Vanilla Extract

PREP
5 MINS

MAKES
ONE

INSTRUCTIONS

1. Place all ingredients in a high speed blender and blend away.
2. Enjoy!

ULTIMATE SUPERFOOD SMOOTHIE

10-oz Coconut Water

1 Frozen Banana

2 Tbsp Cacao Powder

1 Tbsp Maca Powder

1 Tbsp Chia Seeds

1 Tbsp Flax Seeds

1 Tbsp Hemp Seeds

1/2 Cup Frozen Blueberries

2 Tbsp Plant-Based Protein Powder

PREP
5 MINS

MAKES
ONE

INSTRUCTIONS

1. Add all ingredients to a high speed blender and blend until smooth.
2. This recipe makes a phenomenal smoothie bowl as well, just pour into a bowl, top with all your favorite things and extra fresh fruit and enjoy with a spoon!

MINT CHIP SMOOTHIE

1 Frozen Banana
1 Large Handful of Spinach
1/2 Cup Nut Milk of Choice
1/4 tsp Pure Vanilla Extract
1/4 tsp Peppermint Extract

4 Ice Cubes
1/2 Tbsp Cacao Nibs

*Optional Vanilla Plant-Based
Protein Powder

PREP
5 MINS

MAKES
ONE

INSTRUCTIONS

1. Place all ingredients (except cacao nibs) in a high speed blender and blend away.
2. Place the cacao nibs into the blender and pulse once or twice just to break up the nibs and combine everything together. This makes for a nice little chocolate-chip like crunch! Enjoy!

ORANGE CREAMSICLE SMOOTHIE

PREP
5 MINS

2 Cups Freshly Squeezed Orange Juice
1/2 Cup Frozen Mango
1/4 Cup Frozen Pineapple
1/4 Cup Frozen Strawberries

1/2 Tbsp Vanilla Extract

*Optional Vanilla Plant-Based
Protein Powder

MAKES
ONE

INSTRUCTIONS

1. Place everything in a high-speed blender and blend until smooth and creamy.
2. Want to eat this as soft served ice cream?! Just add another 1/4 Cup each of Mango, Pineapple and Strawberries.

RED VELVET SHAKE

PREP
5 MINS

MAKES
ONE

1 Cup Nut Milk of Choice
1 Frozen Banana
1/2 Cup Frozen Cherries
1/4 Cup Fresh Beet
1 Tbsp Cashew Butter
1 tsp Cacao Powder
1/2 tsp Powdered Vanilla (or extract)

*optional:
Add 1/2 Tbsp Cacao Nibs for Extra Crunch
Add a Scoop of Plant-Based Vanilla Protein Powder

INSTRUCTIONS

1. Combine all ingredients (except the cacao nibs) into a high speed blender
2. Blend until smooth.
3. At this point, add your cacao nibs into the blender and pulse once or twice for a pleasant chocolatey chip crunch!

ISLAND GREEN SMOOTHIE

PREP
5 MINS

MAKES
ONE

1 Cup Frozen Pineapple
1 Cup Coconut Milk
2 Cups Spinach, fresh or frozen

1 Packet of Frozen Acai or 2 Tbsp Acai Powder
1 Scoop Vanilla Plant-Based Protein Powder

INSTRUCTIONS

1. Blend everything in a high speed blender until smooth.
2. May need a few extra splashes of milk if using protein.

PB CHOCO-OAT SMOOTHIE

1 Cup Nut Milk of Choice
2 Tbsp Natural Creamy Peanut
Butter
1/4 Cup Dry Oats
1 Frozen Banana

2 Tbsp Cacao Powder
1 tsp Vanilla Extract
Handful of Ice

*Optional: Add 1/2 Tbsp Cacao
Nibs for some extra crunch

PREP
5 MINS

MAKES
ONE

INSTRUCTIONS

1. Combine all ingredients (except the cacao nibs) into a high speed blender
2. Blend until smooth.
3. At this point, add your cacao nibs into the blender and pulse once or twice for a pleasant chocolatey chip crunch!

MANGO MATCHA SMOOTHIE

1 Cup Nut Milk of Choice
1/2 Frozen Banana
1 Cup frozen Mango
2 Medjool Dates, pitted
2 Cups Fresh Spinach

1 tsp Matcha Green Tea Powder
1 tsp Vanilla Extract

*Optional: Add a Scoop of
Vanilla Plant-Based Protein
Powder

PREP
5 MINS

MAKES
ONE

INSTRUCTIONS

1. Blend everything in a high speed blender until smooth.
2. May need a few extra splashes of milk if using protein.

Dressing's & sauces

SIMPLE SALSA

6 Tomatoes, chopped
4 Small Jalapeno
Peppers, minced
1/2 White Onion
1/4 Cup Fresh Cilantro
3 Garlic Cloves
2 tsp Ground Cumin
1 tsp Sea Salt
Juice of 1/2 Lime

PREP
5 MINS

1. Place all ingredients into a food processor and pulse until just combined. (8-10 pulses)
2. Ta-Da done!
3. For best results, make a day ahead of time for best flavor and store in fridge!

PESTO SAUCE

1 Cup Frozen Peas,
defrosted
30 Large Basil Leaves
1/4 Cup Nutritional
Yeast
1/2 tsp Sea Salt
Juice of Half a Lemon
1/2 Avocado
2-3 Tbsp Vegetable
Broth
1 Clove Garlic

PREP
5 MINS

1. Place everything in a food processor and blend starting with just 2 tbsp of vegetable broth and adding more to thin out as needed.
2. Perfect Pesto for pasta-making!

CREAMY RANCH HUMMUS

PREP

5 MINS

1 Can Chickpeas, rinsed and drained
2 Tbsp Tahini
1 Tbsp Apple Cider Vinegar
Juice of 1/2 Lemon
1/4 Cup Water, more if needed
1/2 tsp Sea Salt

3/4 tsp Garlic Powder
1 1/2 tsp Onion Powder
1/2 tsp Dried Parsley
1 tsp Dried Dill
1/2 tsp Dried Basil
1/2 tsp Dried Chives

INSTRUCTIONS

1. Place all ingredients into a food processor.
2. Blend and scrape the processor bowl. Blend and scrape, blend and scrape until nice and smooth.
3. Makes the perfect dip for fresh veggies!

DILL PICKLE HUMMUS

PREP

5 MINS

1 15-oz Can Chickpeas, rinsed and drained
3/4 Cup Dill Pickles, chopped
3 Tbsp Pickle Juice
1/4 Cup Tahini
1 Garlic Clove, chopped
2 Tbsp Fresh Dill

1 Tbsp Freshly Squeezed Lemon Juice
1/2 tsp Sea Salt
2-4 Tbsp Water as Needed

INSTRUCTIONS

1. Place the chickpeas, pickle juice, tahini, garlic, dill, lemon juice and salt into a food processor and blend.
2. Blend and scrape the processor bowl. Add in a few tbsp. of water, one at a time until you get the consistency you desire.
3. Transfer your hummus into a bowl and stir in the chopped pickles with a spatula.

ALFREDO SAUCE

1 Yellow Onion, chopped

1 1/2 Cups Vegetable Broth

1 tsp Sea Salt

1/4 tsp Black Pepper

4 Large Garlic Cloves, minced

1/4 tsp Paprika

1/2 Cup Raw Cashews, soaked overnight, or placed in hot water for 30 minutes

1-2 Tbsp Lemon Juice

1/4 Cup Nutritional Yeast

1/2 Tbsp Arrowroot Flour

INSTRUCTIONS

1. Over Medium-high heat place your chopped onion and just 1 Cup of your vegetable broth into a pan and cook until onions are tender. (about 7 minutes)
2. Add your garlic to the pan and cook for another minute, the broth will be evaporated at this point.
3. Into a high speed blender or food processor, add in your onion garlic mixture along with the rest of the ingredients, using just 1/2 cup of your broth.
4. Blend until smooth.

AVOCADO AIOLI

1 Avocado

1/4-1/3 Cup Aquafaba (liquid from canned chickpeas)

2 Cloves Garlic

Pinch of Cayenne Pepper

Juice of 1/2 Lemon

1/4 tsp Sea Salt

INSTRUCTIONS

1. Place all ingredients into a blender or food processor.
2. Blend and scrape sides to get everything well combined.
3. Store in an air tight container for up to 3 days. (cut recipe in half if you don't plan to use it that fast)

MOZZARELLA CHEESE

1/4 Cup Raw Cashews
(soaked in water
overnight, then
drained)
1 Cup Hot Water
2 Tbsp Arrowroot
Flour
1 Tbsp Nutritional
Yeast
1 Garlic Clove
3/4 tsp Sea Salt
Juice from 1/2 Lemon

PREP
5 MINS

1. Blend all ingredients together in a high speed blender or food processor until smooth.
2. Pour into a saucepan on the stove and cook at a medium heat. Whisk the mixture constantly.
3. After a few minutes it should look like a pot of very gooey melty cheese when it's done.
4. Remove from heat and let cool completely.

NACHO CHEESE SAUCE

2 Medium Red Peppers, roughly chopped
2 tsp Chili Powder
1/2 tsp Cayenne
1/2 tsp Smoked Paprika
1/2 tsp Cumin

1/2 tsp Sea Salt
1/2 Lemon, juiced
1/2 Cup Nutritional Yeast
1/2 Cup Hemp Heart Seeds
2 Garlic Cloves

INSTRUCTIONS

1. Place all ingredients in a high speed blender.
2. Blend until nice and smooth (approx. 30 seconds)
3. You may need to add a tbsp or two of water if your blender isn't as efficient. Note that this sauce will thicken up the longer it sits.

BARBEQUE SAUCE

1 15-oz Can Tomato Sauce
1/4 Cup Apple Cider Vinegar
1/4 Cup Pure Maple Syrup
1/4 Cup Tomato Paste
1/4 Cup Molasses
1 Tbsp Liquid Smoke
1 tsp Smoked Paprika

1 tsp Garlic Powder
1/2 tsp Black Pepper
1/2 tsp Onion Powder
Pinch Ground Cayenne
1/2 tsp Salt

INSTRUCTIONS

1. Place all ingredients in a saucepan on the stove and whisk on medium-high heat. Bring to a simmer then reduce heat to low. Leave the pot uncovered on the stove for 20 minutes. The sauce will be slightly thickened at this point.
2. Let sauce cool completely before storing it in a container.

STRAWBERRY CHIA JAM

2 Cups Fresh
Strawberries
1/4 Cup Pure Maple
Syrup
1 Tbsp Chia Seeds

*Swap the strawberries
for 2 Cups Raspberries
for a Raspberry jam

PREP
15 MINS

1. Dice the strawberries into small pieces.
2. Place the strawberries in a saucepan over medium-high heat along with the maple syrup.
3. Bring to a boil then simmer for about 10 minutes.
4. Stir in the chia seeds and cook for another 5 minutes.
5. After removing from the heat, let the jam cool and thicken.
6. Once cool, place in an air tight container and store in the fridge.
7. The jam will keep well in the refrigerator for 2 to 3 weeks or you can freeze for up to 6 months.

ALMOND-TAHINI DRESSING

2 Tbsp Almond Butter
2 Tbsp Tahini
2 Tbsp Liquid Aminos

1/8 tsp Garlic Powder
1/8 tsp Ground Ginger
1 Tbsp Pure Maple Syrup
2 Tbsp Water

INSTRUCTIONS

Combine all ingredients into a jar or bowl and whisk with a fork until smooth.

AVOCADO-CILANTRO DRESSING

1 Avocado
1/2 Cup Cashews
1/2 Cup Cilantro
1/2-1 Cup Water
Juice of 2 Limes

1 Clove Garlic
1 tsp Chili Powder
1/4 tsp Cayenne
Salt + Pepper to Taste

INSTRUCTIONS

Add all dressing ingredients into a blender (starting with less water and adding more as needed). Blend on high until smooth and creamy.

CAESAR DRESSING

1 Yellow Pepper, roughly chopped
1/2 Cup Hemp Heart Seeds
1/4 Cup Nut Milk of Choice
Juice of Half Lemon
3 Cloves Garlic

2 tsp Dijon Mustard
5 Kalamata Olives
1/4 tsp Sea Salt
Pepper to Taste

INSTRUCTIONS

Add all dressing ingredients into a blender. Blend on high until smooth and creamy.

CREAMY RANCH

1 Cup Soaked Cashews
2 Tbsp Apple Cider Vinegar
Juice of half a lemon
1 tsp Garlic Powder
1/2 tsp Onion Powder
1/2 tsp Dried Parsley
1/2 tsp Dried Chives
1/2 tsp Dried Dill
1/2 tsp Sea Salt
1/2-3/4 Cup Water

PREP
15 MINS

1. Place all ingredients into a high speed blender starting with just 1/2 cup water.
2. Blend until smooth.
3. At this point it will be thicker (great for dipping) but feel free to add more water if you would like a thinner dressing.

Dessert's

PEANUT BUTTER NICE CREAM

3 Frozen Bananas
1/4 Cup Nut Milk of Choice
1 Tbsp Powdered Peanut Butter
*Optional: 1/2 Scoop Vanilla
Plant-Based Protein Powder

PEANUT SAUCE:
2 Tbsp Powdered Peanut
Butter
2 Tbsp Water

TOPPINGS:
Pinch of Sea Salt
1/2 Tbsp Cacao Nibs
1/2 Tbsp Hemp Seeds

PREP
5 MINS

SERVES
ONE

1. Place Bananas, nut milk, 1 Tbsp of powdered peanut butter and optional protein powder to a high speed blender or food processor and blend until smooth.
2. To make the peanut butter sauce, whisk the powdered peanut butter and water together with a fork.
3. Scoop Nice cream into a big bowl and add toppings, sprinkle with salt and drizzle the sauce over top.

PEANUT BUTTER COOKIE DOUGH SUNDAE

3-4 Cookie Dough
Bliss Balls (page 107)
2 Frozen Bananas
2 tsp Vanilla Extract
2 Tbsp Powdered
Peanut Butter
1/4 Cup Nut Milk of
Choice

PREP
5 MINS

SERVES
1-2

1. Blend all ingredients (except the bliss balls) in a high speed blender until smooth.
2. Pour into a large glass and crumble the bliss balls over top and stir them in to disburse the cookie dough throughout your sundae.

CARAMEL BANOFFEE SUNDAE

PREP
10 MINS

SERVES
ONE

INGREDIENTS

2 Frozen Bananas
2 Tbsp Maca Powder
2 tsp Pure Vanilla Extract
1/4 Cup Nut Milk of Choice

1 Cup Prepared Caramel
Popcorn (page 105)
1/4 Cup Prepared Salted
Caramel Sauce (page 163)

INSTRUCTIONS

1. Blend the bananas, maca, vanilla and milk
   in a high speed blender until smooth.
2. Make a little sundae parfait layering the
   ice cream, date sauce and popcorn or pour
   in a bowl and stir the sauce and popcorn
   in and enjoy!

ALMOND SNICKERDOODLES

PREP
10 MINS

COOK
8 MINS

MAKES
18

INGREDIENTS

1 Cup Almond Flour
2 Tbsp Coconut Flour
1/2 tsp Baking Soda
1 tsp Cinnamon
1 Pinch Pink Himalayan Salt
1 Tbsp Coconut Oil, melted
2 Tbsp Almond Butter
1 tsp Lemon Juice
1/4 Cup Pure Maple Syrup
1/2 tsp Vanilla Extract

CINNAMON SUGAR:
1/2 tsp Cinnamon
2 Tbsp Coconut Sugar

INSTRUCTIONS

1. In a large bowl, combine both flours, baking soda, cinnamon, and salt together.
2. In another bowl, whisk together the remaining ingredients.
3. Place your wet ingredients into the dry ingredients and mix together with a spatula until you have a dough ball.
4. Wrap that dough ball into some plastic wrap and place in the fridge for 1 hour.
5. While you are waiting for the cookie dough to chill combine the sugar topping in a small bowl.
6. Unwrap the dough and roll into 1-inch balls, then roll each into the cinnamon sugar.
7. Place each ball on a cookie sheet and flatten the ball just lightly to create a more cookie-like shape.
8. Place in the oven for 8 minutes at 350F.
9. Cool for 15 minutes and enjoy.

CHOCOLATE CHUNK PEANUT BUTTER BROWNIES

PREP
10 MINS

COOK
18 MINS

MAKES
12

INGREDIENTS

1/2 Cup Cacao or Cocoa
Powder
1 Cup Almond Butter
1/2 Cup Unsweetened
Applesauce
2 Tbsp Coconut Oil
(microwave for 15 seconds
just to soften but not melt)
1/4 Cup Pure Maple Syrup
1 1/2 tsp Vanilla Extract
Juice from 1 Lemon
2 Tbsp Chia Seeds
2 Pinches of Sea Salt
1/4 Cup Dairy Free Chocolate
Bar, chopped into chunks (or
your can use Chocolate
Chips)

INSTRUCTIONS

1. Place all ingredients into a bowl of a
   standing mixer (you can also do this by
   hand)
2. With a paddle attachment mix everything
   until you have a smooth batter then add in
   your chocolate chunks (or chips) and mix
   just enough to incorporate.
3. Scoop batter into a glass baking pan and
   bake for 16-18 minutes at 350F. Toothpick
   will come out clean when done.

*Optional: Frost with the "Rich Chocolate
   Frosting" on page 151 for an even richer
   chocolatey brownie

CUPCAKE PERFECTION

PREP
10 MINS

COOK
25 MINS

MAKES
12

INGREDIENTS

1 1/2 Cup Almond Flour
1 Cup Oat Flour
1/2 Cup Coconut Flour
1 tsp Baking Soda
1/2 tsp Sea Salt
1 tsp Xanthan Gum

*Add in 1/4 Cup of Cocoa Powder if you would like chocolate cupcakes. Omit if you just like Vanilla!

1 Tbsp Apple Cider Vinegar
1/3 Cup Coconut Oil, melted
3 tsp Vanilla Extract
1 Cup Agave Nectar Syrup (or maple, but I prefer agave in this one)
1 Cup Water

INSTRUCTIONS

1. In a large bowl, mix together the flours, baking soda, salt and xanthan gum.
2. In another bowl, combine the remaining ingredients together and then add this to the dry ingredients and mix together with a spatula or stand mixer if you like.
3. Scoop the batter into cupcake liners filling only 3/4 of the way up.
4. Bake for 18-25 minutes at 350. A toothpick should come out clean when done.
5. Let cool in the pan for 15 minutes. Then take cupcakes out of the pan and let cool completely before you frost.
6. I highly recommend frosting with either the "Cashew Frosting" on page 151 and add a little acai or dragonfruit powder for some extra color or frost with the "Rich Chocolate Frosting" also on page 151.

To make a cake, just double the recipe and pour into 2-8" round cake pans and bake until toothpick comes out clean!

SILKY CHOCOLATE TARTE

PREP
30 MINS

SERVES
12

INGREDIENTS

CRUST:
Prepared and chilled Easy
Peasy Pie Crust (page 163)
using a 9" pie plate

FILLING:
1 Cup Raw Cashews,
soaked overnight
1/4 Cup Nut Milk of Choice
1/2 Ripe Banana
1 Can Coconut Cream (chill
a can of full fat coconut
milk in the fridge and only
use the cream on top, save
the water at the bottom for
another use, or discard)
2 tsp Vanilla Extract
3 Tbsp Pure Maple Syrup
1/4 Cup Cocoa Powder
1/2 Cup Dairy Free
Chocolate, melted

1 Batch of Chocolate
Ganache (page 162)

INSTRUCTIONS

1. Place the soaked and drained cashews and
   the nut milk into a high speed blender or
   food processor and blend until smooth.

2. Add in the banana, vanilla, coconut cream,
   maple syrup, cocoa and melted chocolate.
   Blend until smooth.

3. Pour the filling out onto the prepared pie
   crust and smooth out. Place this in the fridge
   for 30 minutes to set.

4. Prepare the Chocolate Ganache.

5. Once your pie has set, pour the ganache
   onto the top of the filling and spread out
   evenly.

6. Place the pie in the fridge and let set for an
   hour before serving.

Optional: Add a decorative top
with a batch of Coconut
Whipped Cream (page 162)

PEANUT BUTTER KRISPY BARS

3 Cups Puffed Brown
Rice Cereal
12 Medjool Dates, pitted
3 Tbsp Pure Maple Syrup
3/4 Cup Peanut Butter
1 tsp Vanilla Extract
Pinch of Sea Salt
1 Batch Prepared
Chocolate Ganache
(Page 162)

PREP
10 MINS

SERVES
4-6

1. Combine the dates, syrup, nut butter, and vanilla extract in a
    high speed blender or food processor.
2. Blend until smooth then add to a large bowl.
3. Into the same bowl, add the rice cereal and stir everything
    together.
4. Press the batter firmly into a baking dish lined with
    parchment paper.
5. Place in the refrigerator for an hour.
6. Prepare the chocolate ganache and take bars out of the
    fridge. Pour and spread out the ganache over the bars. Let set
    in the fridge for another 30 minutes then cut and serve.

CASHEW FROSTING

2 Cups Cashews (soaked overnight)
1/3 Cup Nut Milk of Choice
1 tsp Vanilla Extract

1/2 tsp Almond Extract
1/2 Cup Pure Maple Syrup
1/2 tsp Apple Cider Vinegar
1/8 tsp Sea Salt

PREP

35 MINS

INSTRUCTIONS

1. Mix all the ingredients in a high speed blender until creamy. This will take a few minutes to get completely smooth, have patience, it will happen!
2. Taste and add extra sweetener to your liking.
3. Let set in fridge for 30 minutes then frost on anything you like!
4. Add a few Tbsp of acai powder (purple), dragonfruit powder (pink), spirulina (green), for color!

RICH CHOCOLATE FROSTING

1 Ripe Avocado
1/2 Cup Cacao Powder or Cocoa Powder
1/2 Cup Pure Maple Syrup

PREP

10 MINS

INSTRUCTIONS

1. Add all ingredients to a high speed blender or food processor.
2. Blend until smooth.
3. Frost all the things!

PUMPKIN CHOCOLATE CHIP COOKIES

PREP
10 MINS

COOK
10 MINS

MAKES
12

INGREDIENTS

1/2 Cup Solid Coconut Oil
(do not melt)
1/2 Cup Coconut Sugar
1/4 Cup plus 1 Tbsp Pumpkin
Puree
1 tsp Vanilla Extract
1 1/2 Cup Almond Flour
1 Cup Oat Flour
1/4 Cup Coconut Flour
1/2 tsp Sea Salt
1/2 tsp Baking Soda
1/2 tsp Baking Powder
1 1/2 tsp Cinnamon
1/4 tsp Pumpkin Pie Spice
1/2 cup Dairy Free Chocolate
Chips

INSTRUCTIONS

1. In the bowl of a stand mixer using the paddle attachment (or hand mixer), mix together the coconut sugar and oil for 1 minute.
2. Add the pumpkin and vanilla into the sugar and oil and mix.
3. In another bowl, whisk together the flours, salt, baking soda, baking powder, cinnamon, and spices.
4. While the mixer is going, gradually add in all the dry ingredients you whisked together.
5. Lastly add in the chocolate chips and mix throughout the dough with your hands (trust me it's easier with your hands)
6. Roll out your dough (heaping Tbsp) into balls and place on a cookie sheet.
7. Flatten them slightly with your hands to form a cookie shape. (about 1/4 inch thickness)
8. Bake at 350F for 10 minutes
9. Let these cool for 15 minutes before diving in.

CHOCOLATE HAZELNUT MOUSE

PREP
15 MINS

SERVES
4

INGREDIENTS

Liquid from 1 Can of
Chickpeas (Aquafaba)
7-oz Bar of your Favorite
Dark (dairy free) Chocolate
1/3 Cup Nut Milk of your
Choosing
1 Tbsp Pure Maple Syrup
1/2 tsp Hazelnut Extract
Pinch of Sea Salt

INSTRUCTIONS

1. Start by draining a can of chickpeas, saving the liquid from the can.
2. In the bowl of a stand mixer, add the aquafaba and with the wire whisk attachment, (or electric hand mixer) beat on high speed until you get stiff, white peaks (as if you were beating egg whites, cool huh?!)
3. Melt the chocolate and milk together in a double boiler, stirring constantly or in the microwave at 30 second intervals until the chocolate is melted.
4. Transfer the chocolate mixture to a large mixing bowl and whisk in the syrup, extract, and salt.
6. In small batches, fold the whipped aquafaba into the chocolate mixture being very delicate with it.
7. Transfer the mousse into small dishes, then place in the fridge to let the mousse set for at least 4 hours.

LEMON CHEESECAKE

PREP
15 MINS

COOK
1 HOUR

SERVES
12

INGREDIENTS

CRUST:
Prepare the Easy Peasy Pie
Crust on page 163 using a 9"
Round Spring-Form Pan

FILLING:
2 Cups Raw Cashews, soaked
overnight
1 Can Chickpeas, rinsed and
drained
Juice and Zest from 1 Lemon
1 tsp Vanilla Extract
2 Tbsp Arrowroot Flour
1/2 Cup + 2 Tbsp Pure Maple
Syrup
2 Tbsp Cashew Butter
1 Can of Full Fat Coconut Milk
1/2 tsp Sea Salt
3 Tbsp Apple Cider Vinegar

TOPPING OPTIONS:
Strawberry Chia Jam
(page 133)
Coconut Whipped Cream
(page 162)
Salted Caramel Sauce
(page 163)

INSTRUCTIONS

1. Add all the filling ingredients to a high speed blender and blend until completely smooth.
2. Remove crust from the freezer and pour the filling inside and smooth over with a spatula.
3. Bake for 60 minutes at 350F. Check after 60 minutes to see if the filling is set. It should be set around the side and slightly wiggle in the very center like jello, give it a little nudge. If it wiggles throughout, leave in for another 5 minutes and check again until you see that wiggle.
4. Your cheesecake may have cracks, totally normal.
5. Remove from the oven and allow to cool completely, then refrigerate (covered with tin foil) for at least 4 hours or overnight.
6. When ready to serve, remove the spring form ring and top with any of the toppings listed under the "TOPPING OPTIONS".

Tip: For an orange twist,
replace the lemon juice with
fresh
orange juice.

CARROT CAKE

PREP
10 MINS

COOK
55 MINS

SERVES
16

INGREDIENTS

3 Flax Eggs (3 tbsp flax meal
+ 9 tbsp water)
1/3 Cup Melted Coconut Oil
1/2 Cup Pure Maple Syrup
1/4 Cup + 2Tbsp Unsweetened
Apple Sauce
1 tsp Pure Vanilla Extract
1/2 Cup Coconut Sugar
1 tsp Sea Salt
1.5 tsp Baking Soda
1.5 tsp Baking Powder
1 tsp Cinnamon
1 tsp Ground Nutmeg
1/2 tsp Ground Cloves
1 Cup Nut Milk of Choice
1 1/2 Cups Grated Carrots
1 1/2 Cups Almond Flour
1 1/2 Cups Oat Flour
3/4 Cups Raw Walnuts,
Chopped

DECORATE:
1 Batch Cashew Frosting
(page 151)
Chopped Walnuts

INSTRUCTIONS

1. Line two 8-inch cake pans and spray with coconut oil.

2. Prepare flax eggs by adding 9 tbsp of water to 3 tbsp ground flax meal. Stir and set aside to thicken.

3. In a small bowl, whisk together both flours, coconut sugar, baking soda, baking powder, cinnamon, nutmeg, and salt. Set aside.

4. In a bowl of a stand mixer, add the melted coconut oil and maple syrup. Using the whisk attachment, mix together until well-combined. Then add the applesauce, vanilla extract, and flax eggs. Mix well.

5. Alternating the dry ingredients and almond milk, add these slowly to the wet ingredients. Mix until batter is smooth.

6. Fold in the grated carrots and walnuts and mix just until combined.

7. Pour the mixture into the cake pans evenly. Bake for 45-50 minutes until golden brown and a toothpick inserted comes out clean.

8. Allow cakes to cool inside the pans for 15 minutes before removing. Then allow cakes to cool completely on their own before frosting.

PUMPKIN SNICKERDOODLES

PREP
10 MINS

COOK
12-15 MINS

MAKES
12

INGREDIENTS

2 Cups Almond Flour
1/2 tsp Baking Powder
1/2 tsp Pumpkin Pie Spice
1/4 tsp Sea Salt
3 Tbsp Pumpkin
3 Tbsp Melted Coconut Oil
1/4 Cup Maple Syrup
2 tsp Vanilla Extract

CINNAMON SUGAR:
1/2 tsp Cinnamon
2 Tbsp Coconut Sugar

INSTRUCTIONS

1. In a large bowl, whisk together the flour, baking powder, spice and salt.
2. In a second bowl, whisk together the pumpkin, oil, maple syrup and vanilla.
3. Add your wet ingredients into your dry and mix with a spatula until everything is incorporated into a dough.
4. Place dough in the fridge for 15 minutes to chill.
5. Mix the cinnamon and sugar together in another bowl.
6. Once dough has chilled, roll out your dough (heaping Tbsp) into balls, then roll them in the cinnamon sugar.
7. Place each ball on a cookie sheet and flatten them slightly with your hands to form a cookie shape. (about 1/4 inch thickness)
8. Bake at 350F for 12-15 minutes
9. This cookie will come out nice and soft just like your classic snickerdoodle!

COCO-WHIPPED CREAM

PREP
10 MINS

1 Can (14-oz) Full Fat Coconut Milk

1 Tbsp Pure Maple Syrup
1/2 tsp Vanilla Extract

INSTRUCTIONS

1. The night before you plan to make your whipped cream, make sure to put your can of coconut milk in the fridge (should be chilled for at least 10 hours) You can put a mixing bowl in the fridge at the same time to chill.
2. When ready to make, take out the chilled can and mixing bowl. Flip the can over and open it from the bottom with a can opener. Pour out the coconut water (save the water for smoothies mmmm).
3. Scoop the solid coconut cream out and place into the chilled bowl. Using an electric mixer (or hand mixer), beat the cream until fluffy and smooth.
4. Add the syrup and vanilla extract and mix again just to combine. Use the coconut cream immediately or cover and store in the fridge for later (it will firm up if you keep it in the fridge)

CHOCOLATE GANACHE

PREP
10 MINS

2/3 Dairy Free Dark Chocolate or Chocolate Chips

4 Tbsp Full Fat Coconut Milk (from a can)

INSTRUCTIONS

1. Melt the chocolate and coconut milk over a double boiler.
2. Whisk constantly until smooth and melted.

EASY PEASY PIE CRUST

7-8 Medjool dates, pitted
1/2 Cup Oat Flour

1/2 Cup Any Nuts of Your choice (I personally like to mix almonds and hazelnuts)

INSTRUCTIONS

1. Place all the ingredients into a food processor.

2. Pulse the mixture (on, off, on, off) until the mixture is crumbly and moistened.

3. Press the mixture into a pie plate using your fingers or the flat bottom of a cup to evenly spread it out.

4. Place in the freezer for 30 minutes to set, or until you are ready to use it.

SALTED CARAMEL SAUCE

15 Medjool Dates, pitted
3/4 Cup Nut Milk of Choice

3/4 tsp Sea Salt
1 tsp Vanilla Extract

INSTRUCTIONS

1. Place all your ingredients into a high speed blender or food processor.
2. Blend until you have a smooth consistency.
2. Taste and add another 1/4 tsp of salt if you like it saltier.

ACKNOWLEDGEMENTS

First and foremost, thank you to my readers for picking up this book and supporting my dream. It's the comments, messages and photos you send that make my day and keep me motivated and pushing to keep more and more recipes coming.

Thank you to AngelicJewel Photography for the fabulous shot to your left as well as the cover photos. Erin, you always know how to capture exactly what's in my head!

Thank you Dad for letting me borrow your fancy camera for several months and to my Mom for watching Emilia 1 day a week so I could be productive in making this book happen.

And finally, my deepest gratitude to my best friend and partner for life, Shawn Hunt, without whom this book wouldn't have been written. Thank you for being my biggest cheer leader and the person who believed in me as a writer, as a food photographer, as a good cook and baker. Thank you for allowing me to test these recipes out on you night after night until they were just right. I know it was a tough job to fulfill.

As Always,
Go Spread Some Happy, friends!!

CONNECT WITH ME

youtube
@beckybakes

facebook
@beckybakes

instagram
@beckebakes

website
beckyhunt.me

CPSIA information can be obtained
at www.ICGtesting.com
Printed in the USA
BVHW02*1129011018
527582BV00018B/17/P